Albany De Fonblanque

How We Are Governed, or, the Crown, the Senate, and the Bench

A handbook of the constitution, government, laws, and power of Great Britain

Albany De Fonblanque

How We Are Governed, or, the Crown, the Senate, and the Bench
A handbook of the constitution, government, laws, and power of Great Britain

ISBN/EAN: 9783337028701

Printed in Europe, USA, Canada, Australia, Japan

Cover: Foto ©ninafisch / pixelio.de

More available books at **www.hansebooks.com**

HOW WE ARE GOVERNED:

OR,

The Crown, the Senate, and the Bench.

A HANDBOOK

OF

THE CONSTITUTION, GOVERNMENT, LAWS, AND
POWER OF GREAT BRITAIN.

BY

ALBANY FONBLANQUE, Jun., Esq.
OF THE MIDDLE TEMPLE, BARRISTER-AT-LAW.

LONDON:
FREDERICK WARNE AND CO.
BEDFORD STREET, COVENT GARDEN.
1865.

CONTENTS.

LETTER I.
Introduction—Purpose of this Work . . . . p. 1

LETTER II.
THE CONSTITUTION.
The Origin of the British Constitution—Of Parliamentary Government—The Feudal System—Taxation of the Country—Origin of the Houses of Lords and Commons—Parliament—Rights of Englishmen—Habeas Corpus Act—Bill of Rights—Freedom of the Press
pp. 3—15

LETTER III.
THE QUEEN.
The Three Estates of the Realm—Duties of Government—The Royal Office—Succession to the Throne—The Royal Prerogative—The Ministry—The Revenue—The Civil List—The Royal Family—Royal Marriage Act . . . . pp. 16—25

LETTER IV.
THE HOUSE OF LORDS.
The United Parliament—Composition of the House of Lords—Spiritual Peers—Temporal Peers—Rank of Spiritual Peers—Titles and Rank of Temporal Peers—Creation of Peerages—Voting by the Peers—Privileges of the Peerage—The Supreme Court of Appeal
pp. 26—30

LETTER V.
THE HOUSE OF COMMONS.
The Representation of the Country before the Reform Bill—Rotten Boroughs—Party Spirit—An Election under the old System—The present Composition of the House—Qualifications of the Electors—Of the Elected; in Counties; in Boroughs—Proceedings at a Modern Election—The Issuing of the Writ—The Nomination—Show of Hands—The Returning Officer—The Polling—The Return—Rights and Duties of Members . . . . pp. 31—42

LETTER VI.

THE ADVISERS OF THE CROWN.

The Privy Council—The Judicial Committee—The Cabinet Council—The Attorney and Solicitor General—The Ministry, its Composition and Policy—The Opposition . . . . pp 40—48

LETTER VII.

PROCEEDINGS IN PARLIAMENT.

Opening of Parliament—Election and Duties of Speaker—The Speech from the Throne—The Business of Government—Passing Bills, Public and Private—Divisions of the House—Voting by Peers—by the Commons—The Royal Assent—The Budget—Committee of "Ways and Means"—Of Supply—Mutiny Act—Prorogation
pp. 49—58

LETTER VIII.

THE NATIONAL DEBT.

Its Origin—The Funds—Funding System—Transfer of Stock—Price of Money—Reduction of Debt—Sinking Fund—Amount of Debt at various Periods of our History—Revenue—Exports and Imports—Balance of Trade . . . . pp. 59—69

LETTER IX.

LOCAL GOVERNMENT.

Its Principle, Origin, and Objects—High Sheriff and Lord Lieutenant of the County—Local Rates—The Parish and its Officers—The Constable—Churchwardens—Surveyor of Highways—The Vestry, General and Select—The Poor Law—The Law of Settlement—Operation of the Old Poor Law—The New Poor Law—Municipal Corporations—Town Councils—Mayor and Aldermen—Boards of Health—Improvement Commissioners . . . . . . pp. 70—79

LETTER X.

THE CHURCH.

History of the Church of England—Authority of the Pope—The Reformation—Puritans—Roman Catholics—Jews, Disabilities of—Constitution and Discipline of the Church—Bishop—Dean and Chapter—Priest—Deacon—Tithes—Ordinations—Church Accommodation—Convocation . . . . pp. 80—93

CONTENTS.

LETTER XI.

THE ARMY.

Origin and History of Standing Armies—The Feudal System—Mercenary Soldiers—Ancient Warfare—The Mutiny Act—The Secretary for War—The Staff—Cavalry—Infantry—Quartering of Troops—Camps—Purchase System—Price of Commissions—Pay of Officers—Brevet Rank—Recruiting—Pay of Privates—Dragoon Regiments—Names of Regiments—The Royal Artillery—The Royal Engineers—Precedence of Corps—Local Regiments—Courts Martial—Order of the Bath—Victoria Cross—Decorations—Pensions and Rewards—The Militia—The Yeomanry . . pp. 94—121

LETTER XII.

THE NAVY.

Popularity of the Navy—Early History—Naval Ascendancy—Prizes of War—Size of Men-of-War—The Board of Admiralty—Rating of Ships—Officers of a Man-of-War—Stations of Ships—Pay of Officers—Relative Army and Navy Rank—Commissions in the Navy—Pay of Warrant Officers—of Sailors—Pensioners—The Coast Guard—Royal Marines—Pay in the Marines . . . . . . pp. 122—141

LETTER XIII.

THE LAW.

The Common Law—Statute Law—Civil Law—Roman Civil Law—Equity—Conflicts of Law and Equity—New Procedure—Interpretation of the Law—The Sheriff, his Office and Responsibility in executing and enforcing the Law . . . . pp. 142—147

LETTER XIV.

THE COURTS OF LAW AND EQUITY, AND THEIR PROCEDURE.

The Superior Courts—Circuits of the Judges—Their several Commissions—District Courts of Record—Counsel and Attorney—The Inns of Court—An Action at Law—The Pleadings—The Jury—The Trial—The Verdict—Judgment by Default—The Costs—Execution—Judges in Equity . . . . pp. 148—164

LETTER XV.

OF CRIMES AND OFFENCES.

Definition of Crimes—Treasons—Felonies—Misdemeanours—Punishments—Costs of Prosecutions—Accessaries and Accomplices—Nuisances—Common Law Offences . . . . . . pp. 165—175

LETTER XVI.

OF THE COURTS OF CRIMINAL LAW.

The High Court of Parliament—The Court of the Lord High Steward—The Queen's Bench—Office of Coroner—Of Justices of the Peace—The Assize Courts—The Central Criminal Court—Quarter and Petty Sessions—Jurisdiction of Justices of the Peace and Police Magistrates . . . . pp. 170—182

LETTER XVII.

OF THE PRACTICE OF THE CRIMINAL LAW.

Conduct of Public Prosecutions—Arrest of Prisoners by the Police—Examination before Magistrates—Committal or Discharge of Prisoners—Indictments—Office of the Grand Jury—Trial—Challenges of Jurors—Proceedings at Trial—Court of Criminal Appeal—Pardons . . . . pp. 183—199

LETTER XVIII.

LAW OF EVIDENCE.

Conditions of Evidence—Parol—Verbal—Direct—Circumstantial—Primary and Secondary Evidence . . . . pp. 200—204

LETTER XIX.

CONCLUSION . . . . pp. 205—208

HOW WE ARE GOVERNED.

LETTER I.

Introduction—Purpose of this Work.

MY DEAR SON,

You have now reached an age at which it is desirable that you should acquire some knowledge of the institutions under which you have the happiness to live; of the machinery by which the government of the country is conducted; and of the judicial tribunals by which obedience to the law is enforced.

That information I propose to impart to you in a series of letters. I cannot of course enter very minutely into the details of so large a subject. For these I must refer you to other works; but I hope to be able to give you such an outline of our constitutional system as will not only be useful in itself, but will serve as an introduction to the more complete and careful study of this extensive and interesting field of inquiry.

I propose to trace the rise and growth of our mixed constitution; to point out the powers now

INTRODUCTION.

possessed by the different estates of the realm; and to indicate the manner in which they fulfil their functions. I shall devote a letter to the National Debt; and another to the not less important subject of that Local Self-Government, through which so much is done in England that is elsewhere the work of a highly centralized administration. The church, the army and the navy, will each receive due attention; and I shall describe, with as much fulness as my space will permit, the different courts of law and equity, and the methods of procedure in both civil and criminal cases.

You will thus, I trust, be placed in a position to understand the various political questions which you may hear discussed around you, and to appreciate both the substantial merits and the slight defects of a system, which has been formed by the persevering and patriotic efforts of many generations of Englishmen and under which the British empire has come to be what we see it to-day—the envy and admiration of less fortunate nations.

Your affectionate father,
A. B.

LETTER II.

THE CONSTITUTION.

The Origin of the British Constitution—Of Parliamentary Government—The Feudal System—Taxation of the Country—Origin of the Houses of Lords and Commons—Parliament—Rights of Englishmen—Habeas Corpus Act—Bill of Rights—Freedom of the Press.

THIS Letter must be considered as a sort of introduction to those which follow; and in it I am obliged to depart from the rule of confining myself to treating of our institutions as they now exist for reasons which you will very soon perceive.

The "constitution" of a country is the established system under which its government is conducted. It is defined by Paley to be "so much of its law as relates to the designation and power of the legislature; the rights and functions of the several parts of the legislative body; the construction, office, and jurisdiction of courts of justice."

The origin of the British Constitution is hidden amidst the general obscurity which surrounds the early history of our ancestors. Harassed as they were by repeated invasions, and unsettled by consequent changes amongst their rulers, they have left us a very indistinct idea of the manner in which the business of their government was carried on. The principle, however, which guided it is clear; for from a period long before the union of the states of the Heptarchy under one crown, the sway of their princes was assisted, and in some measure controlled, by assemblages of their people, which may be taken to be the origin of the parliaments of the present day.

These assemblages were known under various names. In Saxon, as the *Michel Gemote*, or *Great Meeting;* the *Michel Synod*, or *Great Council;* and the *Wittena Gemote*, or *Meeting of Wise Men.* After the consolidation of the seven kingdoms the united council was called in Latin *Commune Concilium Regni*, the Common Council of the Kingdom; *Magnum Concilium Regis*, "the Great Council of the King;" *Curia Magna*, "the Great Court;" and in other languages by other similar designations, which I need not enumerate. This council not only made and altered the laws of the land; but also enforced them, being a court of justice for settling disputes relating to the ownership of land, and for trying and punishing great criminals. It also imposed the taxes, and sometimes appointed the king's ministers. By an ordinance of Alfred the Great, it was commanded to assemble twice in the year at least, or oftener, according to the state of the country; and the laws which it passed were prefaced with a declaration that they were such as the king, with the advice of his clergy and wise men, had instituted. You will perceive hereafter how close a resemblance this ancient council bears to the modern Parliament.

Shortly after the Norman Conquest the *feudal system*, at that time in force throughout a great portion of Europe, was introduced into England by William the Norman; not, as is sometimes said, to enable him to reward his followers out of the spoils of a conquered country, but at the request of the Great Assembly of the Realm, in order that the kingdom might be put into a state of defence against a threatened invasion from Denmark. Once established, however, by the people for their protection against a foreign enemy, it was soon turned against them by those to whom they looked for protection into an engine of the grossest oppression. Under this feudal system (which, in its purity, was admirably adapted to an age in which war and conquest were the chief pursuits of mankind) the entire soil of a country was held to be the absolute property of its sovereign; and was divided into estates called *feuds* or *feofs*, and held of him by his chief men, called the *barons, vassals,* and *ten-*

ants in capite of the Crown, upon the condition of their doing homage and swearing *fealty* (loyalty) to him, and attending him in his wars at the head of a certain number of armed men. To obtain these they in turn had to distribute land, and also to let out their own estates for cultivation in their absence, whilst performing their services, receiving *rent* (called in those days *redditus*, or a return) in the shape of corn and provisions to support them and their followers upon their campaigns. The relationship this created was known as that of *lord* and *vassal*. Every vassal was bound to defend and obey his immediate lord, according to the terms under which he held his land, but no further. On his part the lord was bound to protect his vassals, and to do justice between them.

At first these *feuds* were held only during the will of the lord; they could not be transferred or disposed of by those who held them during their lives, nor did they descend to their heirs at their deaths. Those persons only who were capable of bearing arms, and were chosen by the lord, could succeed to them. Infants, women, and monks, were, therefore, excluded as a matter of course. Subsequently, the heirs of a deceased tenant were permitted to share his lands amongst them upon payment of what was called a *fine*, or present of armour, horses, or money to the lord. But the division of authority this occasioned was found to weaken the defences of the country; and it became the general rule to admit one heir only, in some parts the eldest, in others the youngest son of the deceased, or some other male relative capable of taking upon himself the conditions of the feud. Gradually, as intelligence and wealth began to increase, and other arts than those of war to be followed, these feuds became the absolute property of their tenants—no longer *vassals* liable to be dispossessed at any moment at the mere caprice of the lord, but *free holders* of the soil, possessing power to sell or bequeath it as they pleased, subject only to known rules of law, which in every succeeding reign were relaxed in their favour.

The changes which in a few lines I have thus narrated to you took many eventful years to accomplish. Our sturdy forefathers grappled manfully with the iron yoke to which they had unwittingly subjected themselves, and slowly, but surely, regained the freedom which had been enjoyed under their old Saxon rulers. Their kings frequently required, for furthering their ambition or ministering to their pleasure, larger sums and greater services than the feudal-system could provide; and, as it was a fixed principle in this country, in its earliest days and under its most despotic rulers, that no man should be taxed without his own consent or that of his representative, the Great Council of the nation—the successor of the *Wittena Gemote*—had to be summoned to grant what was required. Seldom did it do so without obtaining in return the abolition of some abuse, or the restoration of some privilege as the price of its concessions.

For a considerable time this council consisted of all the king's *barons*, or those who held estates immediately of the Crown; but its constitution was regulated by Magna Charta, which ordained (amongst other things) that all archbishops, bishops, abbots, earls, and greater barons should be summoned to Parliament severally by the king's letters. Thus what we now call the House of Lords was established.

In time of peace the great barons resided in castles scattered throughout the country, in which they held almost regal state and exercised almost royal powers. The lower orders flocked beneath their battlements for protection against robbers and the followers of other lords hostile to their own; for these barons were a lawless, turbulent race, and often at open war with each other. Thus, in many places, as population increased, towns were formed. There are few old cities and towns in England in the midst of which you will not see the ruins of some castle or fortress frowning from an eminence, or guarding the banks of a river; and round its crumbling walls are sure to be found the oldest houses in the place. As arts, commerce, and trade began to take root and flourish, the inhabitants of some of these settlements became so enriched as to be able to purchase great privileges of their immediate lords, and of the king, which rendered them independent communities. Soon, therefore, owing to the old principle which I have mentioned, it became necessary to summon some of their members to the Great Council, not as barons, but as *citizens* and *burgesses*. For similar reasons the freeholders, whose progress from a state of servitude I have already sketched, had to be represented by *knights of the shire*, elected from amongst themselves, to enable the king to collect revenue from their rich brethren. The exact date at which our Constitution took this shape is the subject of much doubt; but it is certain that in the reign of Henry III., Simon de Montford, Earl of Leicester, and the king's minister, issued writs directing the election of two knights for every county, two citizens for every city, and two burgesses for every borough, to serve in the grand council of the kingdom. In the reign of Edward III. the laws were declared to be made with the consent of the "*commonalty*," which by a royal charter is then acknowledged as an "estate of the realm ;" and subsequently by a statute passed in the twenty-fifth year of the reign of the same monarch it was declared "that no taleage or aid shall be taken without the goodwill and consent of the archbishops, earls, barons, knights, burgesses, and *other freemen of the land.*" I have quoted this to show from what classes the consent was to be obtained; the principle which it confirms is, as I have said, of much older date. Thus was the power of the Commons acknowledged as a governing body in the State.

It was some time before the Lords and the Commons were placed apart in separate chambers, and made distinct councils, each guided by rules, and performing duties, of its own, as we now find them. At first they sat together in one assembly; and although the laws that they made applied to the kingdom at large, each body taxed itself, and had no voice in fixing what should be paid by the other. The taxation of the country is now entirely managed by the House of Commons.

For many years Parliament was made use of by

our kings as a mere instrument for taxing the people. It was called together when money was wanted, and dissolved as soon as the requisite supplies were granted. Sometimes it refused to fill the king's purse until some harsh usage was repealed, some old custom restored, or the royal assent given to some new law; but many generations passed away before it began to make and alter the laws as part of its regular duties.

I have followed the progress of parliamentary government so far, to account to you for the shape in which we now find it, not to supply a history of its rise. I will now give you a brief summary of the rights and privileges which, during the periods that I have passed over, our forefathers won for us, and which we now enjoy.

Every subject of the United Kingdom is born free. He cannot be sold as a slave; neither can he be put to death, banished, removed, or imprisoned, except by the judgment of a court of justice. He has a right to live in his country wherever he pleases, and to leave it when he chooses. His property cannot be interfered with except by operation of law. He may petition the sovereign, or Parliament. He may appeal to the law, and its remedies cannot be denied to him. By the famous statute, called the " Habeas Corpus Act," any person who is imprisoned or kept under improper control may obtain a writ which entitles him to be taken into open court, there to learn the reason of his imprisonment or detention; and if he can show that he is improperly deprived of his liberty, he is entitled to be discharged from custody. Under the equally famous Bill of Rights (passed shortly after the accession of William and Mary to the throne vacated by James II.), the authority of Parliament and the freedom of the subject is confirmed in the following terms. It is declared—

1. That the pretended power of suspending laws, or the execution of laws, by regal authority, without consent of Parliament, is illegal.

2. That the pretended power of dispensing with laws, or the execution of laws, by regal authority, as it hath been assumed and exercised of late, is illegal.

3. That the commission for erecting the late Court of Commissioners for Ecclesiastical Causes (the Court of High Commission, founded by James II.), and all other commissions or courts of like nature, are illegal and pernicious.

4. That levying money for, or to the use of the Crown, by pretence of prerogative without grant of Parliament, for longer time or other manner than the same is or shall be granted, is illegal.

5. That it is the right of the subject to petition the king; and all commitments and prosecutions for such petitioning are illegal.

6. That the raising or keeping a standing army within the kingdom, in the time of peace, unless it be with consent of Parliament, is against law.

7. That subjects which are Protestants may have arms for their defence suitable to their conditions, and as allowed by law. (This section now extends to all denominations of her Majesty's subjects, the oppressive laws relating to the Roman Catholics having been repealed.)

8. That election of members of Parliament ought to be free.

9. That the freedom of speech and debates or proceedings in Parliament ought not to be impeached or questioned in any court or place out of Parliament.

10. That excessive bail ought not to be required, nor excessive fines, nor cruel and unusual punishments inflicted.

11. That jurors ought to be duly impanelled and returned; and jurors who pass judgment upon men in trials for high treason, ought to be freeholders.

12. That all grants and promises of fines and

forfeitures of particular persons, before conviction, are illegal and void.

13. That, for redress of all grievances, and for the amending, strengthening, and preserving of the laws, parliaments ought to be held frequently.

No mention of the freedom of the press is made in this celebrated declaration. Our press is now absolutely free; no permission is required for the publication of any news, or any comments upon it. The conduct of the highest in the land may be praised or censured as their merits deserve—care only must be taken that no untrue or malicious statements are made, by means of which public peace and morality, or private character may suffer; but even when such are put forward, they cannot be suppressed by any arbitrary exercise of authority. Like every other wrong, they must be submitted to a court of law, and by the judgment of a court of law alone can their authors be punished.

"To submit the press," says BLACKSTONE, in his *Commentary upon the Law of England,* "to the restrictive power of a licenser, as was formerly done both before and since the Revolution (and is now done in almost every continental State), is to subject all freedom of sentiment to the prejudices of one man, and to make him the arbitrary, infallible judge of all controverted points in learning, religion, and government. But to punish (as the law does at present) any dangerous or offensive writings which, when published, should, on fair and impartial trial, be adjudged of a pernicious tendency, is necessary for the preservation of peace and good order of government and religion, the only solid foundations of civil liberty."

My reason for introducing this important subject in this Letter may be gathered from the celebrated words of Mr. Canning, who said that, " He who, speculating on the British Constitution, should omit from his enumeration the mighty powers of public opinion embodied in a free press, which pervades and checks, and perhaps in the last resort nearly governs the whole, would give but an imperfect view of the government of England."

LETTER III.

THE QUEEN.

The Three Estates of the Realm—Duties of Government—The Royal Office—Succession to the Throne—The Royal Prerogative—The Ministry—The Revenue—The Civil List—The Royal Family—Royal Marriage Act.

HAVING now laid the foundation of my subject, I shall proceed to show you how this country is governed at the present day.

The United Kingdom of Great Britain and Ireland is governed by its King or Queen and two Houses of Parliament. These are known as the Three Estates of the Realm.

The duties of government are to make, and put in force, the laws of the country for its own people as subjects, and to represent them as a nation in their dealings with foreign powers. The first of these duties—*the making* of the law—is performed by the three Estates conjointly; the remainder belong to the sovereign alone. I shall devote a Letter to each of the three Estates, and in this will tell you of

THE SOVEREIGN.

There is no difference between the power exercised by a king and a queen in this country. Their office is hereditary, passing upon the death of the sovereign to the next heir—males, in the same degree of relationship, being preferred to females: thus the youngest son of the present sovereign would inherit the throne to the exclusion of her eldest daughter, but any daughter would stand in the order of succession before an uncle, a nephew, or a male cousin.

The succession to the throne of the United Kingdom of Great Britain and Ireland was regulated in the commencement of the reign of William III. by an act of Parliament called the "Act of Settlement," by which the Roman Catholic branch of the family of the Stuarts was formally excluded from the succession. By this act, the sovereign power was limited to the heirs of the Princess Sophia of Brunswick (the granddaughter of James I.), being Protestants. Upon the death of Queen Anne, the son of this princess, King George I., became king. He was succeeded by his son, George II. From him the crown descended to his grandson, George III., and from him to his son, George IV.; who, dying without issue surviving, was succeeded by his brother, William IV.; upon whose death, having left no children, the daughter of his next younger brother, the Duke of Kent, her present most gracious Majesty Queen Alexandrina Victoria, ascended the throne.

The crown of these kingdoms can only be worn by a Protestant. Should the king or queen marry a Roman Catholic, it is forfeited from that moment. Nor can any member of the Royal family, who is married to a Roman Catholic, ascend the throne.

The person of the sovereign is sacred; she is above the law; no act of Parliament can bind her, unless it contain express words to that effect. It is also a maxim of the law that she can do no wrong; she is not responsible for the commission of any act, and no omission upon her part can be taken advantage of; she possesses the power of pardon and of mercy towards criminals; she is the fountain of justice and of honour; from her all titles of nobility and honourable distinctions spring; all military and civil rewards and decorations, such as orders of knighthood, crosses, stars, and medals for meritorious services, are in her gift, and no subject may wear or assume one granted by a foreign prince without her license. All commissions to officers in the army and navy are granted, although they are not now signed, by her; she has the power of proroguing Parliament —that is, putting an end to its sittings for a time, and of dissolving it and convoking a new one in its place; she is the supreme head of the State, the Church, the Army, and the Navy; she has the power of sending and receiving ambassadors, of declaring war and making peace, of arranging treaties, and coining money for the use of her subjects; she may refuse her assent to laws passed by the two Houses of Parliament, but has no direct voice in discussing them, speaking only through her ministers.

These, and other rights, are called the *prerogative of the Crown.*

Under the British Constitution the sovereign must govern through her ministers, who are responsible to Parliament and the country for her political acts, which are always presumed to be done by their advice. No ministry is able to carry on the business of the country for more than a very short time, unless it can obtain the assent of Parliament to its proceedings. Of late years the great political questions, upon which the formation and existence of ministries have depended, have been discussed and settled in the House of Commons. This Estate of the realm being elected by the people, you will perceive that the ministry, although *nominally* appointed by the Crown, is *virtually* chosen by the country. Should the ministry or Parliament attempt to interfere improperly with the royal prerogative, the sovereign can dismiss the one, and dissolve the other. Should a faction in Parliament oppose the ministry in doing what they and the queen consider to be for the welfare and honour of the country, the opinion of all classes can be taken by summoning a new Parliament. Should the Crown and the ministry set themselves against Parliament and the people, the former, by refusing to grant supplies for the public service, could secure the dismissal of the obnoxious advisers. Thus a balance of power is preserved between the Estates of the realm, which prevents any one of them from infringing the rights of the others, and makes the people of this country the happiest, the freest, and at the same time the most loyal, nation under the sun.

In former times, the taxes which were granted by Parliament were handed over to the king, to be expended by him in maintaining his state, and for keeping up the military and naval services. He had also estates in various parts of the country called the *crown lands*, the rents and profits of which were paid into his treasury. The *revenue*, or annual income of the country derived from the taxes imposed by Parliament and the income from these estates (with the exception of the duchy of Lancaster, which belongs to her Majesty not as Queen of England, but as Duchess of Lancaster), is now collected into one fund called the *Consolidated Fund*. The first charge upon this fund is the payment of interest upon the national debt

THE CIVIL LIST.   21

called the *funds*, and upon the *unfunded debt* The origin and progress of the national debt is so important and interesting a subject, that I shall devote to it a future Letter.

The next charge upon the Consolidated Fund brings me back to the subject which I have quitted for a moment. It is an allowance called the *civil list*, apportioned to the queen for the support of her household and the dignity of her crown. This was fixed by the statute 1st Victoria, cap. 11, at 385,000*l.*, to be paid annually, and appropriated as follows: Her Majesty's privy purse, 60,000*l.*; salaries of her Majesty's household and retired allowances, 131,000*l.*; expenses of the household, 172,500*l.*; royal bounty and special services, 13,200*l.*; pensions, 1,200*l.*; and miscellaneous, 8,040*l.* On the Consolidated Fund are likewise charged the following sums, allowed to members of the Royal family, namely—8,000*l.* to the Princess Frederick William of Prussia; 6,000*l.* to the Princess Louis of Hesse Darmstadt; 6,000*l.* to the Duchess of Cambridge; 6,000*l.* to her daughter, the Grand-Duchess of Mecklenburg-Strelitz; 3,000*l.* to the Princess Mary of Cambridge, and 12,000*l.* to the Duke of Cambridge. The Prince of Wales has an annuity of 40,000*l.*, payable out of the Consolidated Fund, settled upon him. He has, also, the revenues of the Duchy of Cornwall, which now amount to about 50,000*l*. a year, with every prospect of their increasing. The Princess of Wales has settled upon her by Parliament the annual sum of 10,000*l*., to be increased to 30,000*l*. in case of widowhood. The sum for carrying on the civil government, including the salaries of the ministers of state, judges, and others, is also charged upon the Consolidated Fund, the remainder of which is paid into the exchequer, for the public service, to defray the expenses of our army, navy, civil service, &c. &c.

All the great officers of state, the bishops, and judges, the officers in the army and navy, are appointed by the queen, or in her name; but as the ministry is responsible for the fitness of the persons appointed, and for their conduct whilst in the public service, the selection is placed in their hands, and the sovereign approves, almost as a matter of course, of the person recommended.

Before I conclude, it would be as well were I to tell you something about the royal family.

The royal consort—that is, the wife or husband of a king or queen—has, as such, no share in the government of the country. They are subjects of the Crown only, and may be appointed to fill any post in the state that a subject can hold. A queen consort has some special privileges and protections. She can sue and be sued in all courts of justice as though she were an unmarried woman; and for this purpose she has her own attorney and solicitor-general to conduct her law business. She has power to purchase lands and to convey—that is, dispose of—them. She can take a legal grant from her husband, and make a will; no other married women can do these things. She has a separate household and officers of state. Her person, like the king's, is sacred.

A queen *dowager* is the widow of a king.

The Prince of Wales is the eldest son of the sovereign, and heir-apparent to the Crown. He is created Prince of Wales and Earl of Chester and Dublin, and is born Duke of Cornwall. He is also High Steward of Scotland, Duke of Rothsay, Earl of Carrick, Baron of Renfrew, and Lord of the Isles. His person and that of his wife are specially protected by the law. Should the eldest son die, his next brother becomes Prince of Wales and Earl of Chester, but not Duke of Cornwall.

The Princess Royal is the eldest daughter of the sovereign. Her person is also specially protected, as, should no son be born or live to succeed to the crown, she would become queen.

The other members of the royal family have no

special rights conferred by law. They rank before all dukes, and are forbidden by the statute 12 Geo. III. c. 11, called the *Royal Marriage Act*, to marry without the consent of the sovereign signified under the great seal; but it is provided that such of the descendants of George II. "as are above the age of twenty-five may, after a twelve-month's notice given to the King's Privy Council, contract and solemnize marriage without the consent of the Crown, unless both Houses of Parliament shall, before the expiration of the said year, expressly declare their disapprobation of such intended marriage." Persons assisting, or being present, at a prohibited marriage incur very heavy penalties. The act I have quoted does not affect the children of princesses married into foreign families.

From this general sketch of the prerogatives of the Crown, and the position of the Royal family, you will understand what is meant by saying that England is under a "limited monarchy." The sovereigns of other countries often assert a "divine right" to govern; a sovereign of the house of Hanover can put forth no such pretensions, because he holds his crown under, and by virtue of, the act of settlement, and strictly subject to the conditions which it imposes. But although the direct power of the monarch be small, his indirect influence is considerable. His personal predilections are not without weight in determining which of the leading statesmen of the predominant political party shall fill the post of first minister; and, as the head of English society, he can materially influence the tone of manners and morals, and either promote or retard the progress of social improvement.

LETTER IV.

THE HOUSE OF LORDS.

The United Parliament—Composition of the House of Lords—Spiritual Peers—Temporal Peers—Rank of Spiritual Peers—Titles and Rank of Temporal Peers—Creation of Peerages—Voting by the Peers—Privileges of the Peerage—The Supreme Court of Appeal.

THE House of Lords or Peers, or, as it is also called, the Upper House of Parliament, ranks next in dignity to the Crown, as the second Estate of the realm. Its origin I have already traced in my Introductory Letter.

Before their respective union with England, Ireland and Scotland had each a parliament, and consequently a House of Lords of its own. Now, however, there is but one House for the United Kingdom, and only a certain number of peers selected from the nobility of the sister countries have seats in it. The members of the peerage of Scotland and Ireland who have not seats in Parliament enjoy every other privilege of their order. Peers of Scotland are no longer created; but for every three Irish peerages that become extinct—that is, have no one capable of inheriting them—the Queen has the power of creating one new one. There is no limit to the number of British peers that she may make.

The following is a summary of the members of the House of Lords in the session of 1864:—

SPIRITUAL PEERS.

2 Archbishops of England and Wales.
24 Bishops   do.   do.
1 Archbishop of Ireland, elected each session.
3 Bishops of Ireland   do.   do.

Total, 30

I will tell you how Bishops are appointed in my Letter upon THE CHURCH.

TEMPORAL PEERS.

H.R.H. the Prince of Wales.
2 Royal dukes.
20 Dukes.
19 Marquises.
110 Earls.
22 Viscounts.
209 Barons.
28 Peers of Ireland, elected for life.
16 Peers of Scotland, elected for each parliament.

Total, 427

30 Spiritual peers.
427 Temporal peers.

Grand total, 457

The Archbishop of Canterbury takes rank next after the youngest royal duke; the Archbishops of York and Armagh, in the order of their consecration, next but one, the Lord Chancellor intervening. The bishops rank as barons at the head of that order, those of London, Durham, and Winchester taking precedence of all other English—and the Bishop of Meath of all other Irish—bishops. The Queen may appoint as many bishops as she may be advised, but thirty only have seats in Parliament. They are said to sit, not by virtue of their sacred office, but as barons in respect of the temporal estates attached to their sees; but some difference of opinion is felt by learned persons upon this point. I will tell you how bishops are appointed, in my letter upon THE CHURCH.

The temporal peers rank in the order in which I have placed them in the above table, those in the same degree of nobility taking precedence according to the date of their creation.

The title of DUKE is derived from the Latin word *dux*, a leader.

The title of MARQUIS was conferred upon those who held the command of the *Marches*, as the boundaries between England and Wales, and England and Scotland, were called when those countries were hostile to this nation.

The title of EARL is derived from the Saxon word *eorl*, noble. The earl formerly had the government of a *shire*. After the Conquest, earls were called counts, and from them their shires have taken the name of *counties*.

The VISCOUNT, *Vice-comes*, was the deputy of the earl.

The title of BARON is the oldest in point of antiquity, although the lowest in point of rank, of any order of nobility. He was, as I have already stated, one who held estates immediately of the king.

Peers are now created by *letters-patent* from the Crown. Formerly a writ of summons, calling upon the persons intended to be ennobled, to take their place in the House of Lords, was issued; and thus they became peers of Parliament. Writs of summons are now issued when it is intended to call the eldest son of a peer to the House of Lords in the lifetime of his father.

The House of Lords is usually presided over by the Lord Chancellor; but he does not decide, as does the Speaker of the House of Commons, upon the regularity of its proceedings. The House at large does this; and members whilst delivering their speeches address the assembly and not the Lord Chancellor, or other lord upon the woolsack.

Peers vote either in person—using the words *content* or *non content*, to signify their approval or rejection of the question before them—or by *proxy*—a signed paper to the same effect used upon their behalf, in their absence, by some other peer. They have also the privilege of entering a *protest* in the *Journals* of the House against any proceeding resolved upon by it against their will. They have the right of audience with the sovereign at all times. All laws relating to the rights of their order must be originated in the House of Lords; and all disputed claims to titles of nobility are referred by the Crown to it for decision. They cannot be arrested for debt. The House of Lords is the proper tribunal for trying persons impeached by the House of Commons; it also has the right of trying its own members when accused of treason or felony. To assist it in these duties, the judges and law officers of the Crown have writs *ad consultandum* (to consult), and are its legal advisers. Finally, as the supreme court of justice in the kingdom, it is the last tribunal of appeal from the judgments of the other courts; but, practically speaking, this jurisdiction is not exercised by the House as a body, but by such of its members, as hold, or have held, high judicial offices.

LETTER V.

THE HOUSE OF COMMONS.

The Representation of the Country before the Reform Bill—
Rotten Boroughs—Party Spirit—An Election under the old
System—The present Composition of the House—Qualifica-
tions of the Electors—Of the Elected : in Counties ; in
Boroughs—Proceedings at a modern Election—The issuing
of the Writ—The Nomination—Show of Hands—The Re-
turning Officer—The Polling—The Return — Rights and
Duties of Members.

THE House of Commons, or Lower House, consists of persons chosen by the people to represent them in Parliament.

I have already told you its origin, and why its members were assembled. The number of places to be represented and of the members that they were entitled to return was originally fixed by the kings ; and as they looked with great jealousy upon the increasing power of Parliament, no additions of any great importance were made as the wealth and population of the country began to expand. A history of the progress of the House of Commons would be, in fact, a history of England, and with that I have no intention to supply you. I need only tell you that the acts of union with Scotland and Ireland fixed the numbers of members to be sent by each part of the United Kingdom, and that our representative system, as it now exists, was settled by the Reform Bill passed in the year 1832.

Before the passing of this measure—which we owe to the perseverance, ability, and statesmanship of Earl (then Lord John) Russell and the late Lord Grey—an election was a very different affair to what it is now. In the first place, party spirit ran to a height which the better sense of the present day would not tolerate, and can scarcely realize. In many towns, a Whig would not sit down to the same table with a Tory, and their respective wives and families would not show common civility to each other when they were thrown in contact, merely because they happened to differ in politics! Many large counties, such as Cheshire, Lancashire, Surrey, and Cornwall, which now return four members to Parliament sent but two; whilst towns of considerable commercial importance, such as Manchester, Halifax, and Birmingham, were not represented at all. On the other hand, numbers of petty places—belonging to some nobleman or rich country gentleman—of no political or commercial importance whatever, and containing not more than a score or so of voters, and often less, returned their one or two members to Parliament. These were called *rotten boroughs*, and those who owned and supported them *boroughmongers*. The party in opposition to these were *reformers*. The proprietor of a rotten borough returned whom he pleased; himself, or his son, or nephew, or, if these were not of sufficient age, some obliging friend who would continue its member until they attained years of discretion, when he would retire in their favour.

In counties where some great landowner was supreme, or a combination of landowners holding the same politics prevailed, the same thing was done. But in others, where the interests were divided, the fiercest contests took place. The voting began at nine o'clock in the morning, and continued till four o'clock in the afternoon, and went on day after day, provided that a vote were recorded every hour, until the whole of the electors had polled. Thus you may easily perceive that in a constituency of several thousands the contests might be kept up for months. And so they were; the question in dispute being not who was the best men to send to Parliament, but which side would spend the most money. The most wholesale bribery went on openly, or was administered under the flimsy pretext of giving employment to electors as agents, messengers, banner bearers, and the like, at wages out of all proportion to their labours. The electors who had voted were entertained, with a view to securing their suffrages on some future occasion: those who had not, were lodged and feasted, in order that the other side might not obtain their votes. The more protracted the struggle the more money would be spent by both parties, and the better would it be for the electors. Bands of prize-fighters and other ruffians were hired by rival candidates to uphold their cause and intimidate the weak and unprotected. Drunkenness and every species of debauchery reigned paramount. Electors were kidnapped by the opposing party for fear they should vote, or locked up by their friends for fear they should be kidnapped. Hundreds and thousands of pounds were spent in carrying out these disgraceful tactics; and the resources of many a noble family were sadly crippled by the enormous outlay required. It is reported that the costs of a celebrated contested election in Leicestershire resulted in a permanent charge of 15,000*l.* a year upon the estate of the successful candidate!

Wide and decisive as were the remedies supplied by the Reform Bill to this state of affairs, I cannot say that they were administered with a thoroughly impartial hand. The rotten boroughs in the hands of the Tories were swept away, but many that were at the disposal of the Whigs (the party then in power) were suffered to exist. Still it was a great reform, and the Act, when passed, was looked upon as a conclusive measure. It is now, however, generally conceded that in order to keep pace with the growing population, wealth, and intelligence of the day, a further extension and purification of our representative system must very soon take place.

The House of Commons consists at present (1865) of 658 members. Of these England and Wales is represented by 500; Ireland, by 105; and Scotland, by 53. Members are elected for counties, cities, and boroughs, and for the Universities of Oxford, Cambridge, and Dublin. Some large counties, such as Yorkshire, are divided, each division returning its own members. The right of choosing Members of Parliament is termed the *elective franchise*, and those who exercise it are called electors.

An acquaintance with the law relating to the tenure of land is requisite to enable you exactly to understand the sort of qualification required of electors in counties; I may, however, briefly state that in England all persons who possess an estate of the value of 40s. belonging to themselves and their heirs for ever, or who hold one of the lord of a manor of the value of 10*l*. a year during their own lives or for the life of another person, or who rent other land of that value for sixty years, or who occupy an estate for which they pay 50*l*. a year, are entitled to vote.

In cities and boroughs in England the tenants of houses or holdings of the clear annual value of 10*l*., and persons claiming privileges, which I need not describe, as *freemen* and *burgesses*, are electors.

Ireland and Scotland have each a separate law regulating the qualifications of electors.

The degree of Master of Arts, without any property qualification, confers a vote in the universities.

Such are the qualifications of electors. The following are *dis*qualifications. No person can vote who

1. Is an alien or foreigner.
2. Has not arrived at the age of 21 years.
3. Has been convicted of perjury in a court of law.
4. Has been in receipt of parochial relief during the year.
5. Is concerned or employed in the charging, collecting, levying, or managing the duties of customs or excise, or in collecting the house duty.

DISQUALIFICATIONS OF CANDIDATES. 37

6. Who is employed under the Commissioners of Stamps, or is such commissioner.

7. Who is employed in any way connected with the General Post Office, or is a police constable.

8. Who is a peer of the realm; and

9. Who has been convicted of bribery, treating, or using undue influence at an election.

In every county, city, and borough a register of qualified voters is kept. This list is *revised* once every year by barristers appointed for that purpose, when the names of persons who have become entitled to vote are entered, and the names of those who have died or become disqualified are struck out.

Until the year 1858 members of the House of Commons were required to possess a property of a certain value; but in that year this qualification was abolished. The following, however, are disqualified by law:

1. Aliens.

2. The fifteen judges of the superior courts, of common law, the lords justices, the three vice-chancellors, the judges of the county courts, police magistrates, and revising barristers.

3. Persons under the age of twenty-one years.

4. Clergymen—Protestant and Roman Catholic.

5. Outlaws in criminal cases, and persons convicted of treason and felony.

6. Candidates reported guilty of bribery or treating at an election (disqualified only for the existing parliament).

7. The returning officer of the county, city, or borough of which he is such officer.

8. Persons concerned in the management of taxes created since 1692, or holding places of profit under the Crown created since 1718.

9. Pensioners of the Crown.

and lastly

10. Army agents, government contractors, and sheriffs' officers.

Seven years is the limit fixed by law for the duration of any parliament, at the end of that period it becomes dissolved as a matter of course. It is also dissolved six months after the death of the Sovereign, and may, as has already been said, be put an end to at any moment by the exercise of the royal authority.

When a new Parliament has to be called together, a royal warrant is directed to the Lord Chancellor, ordering him to cause the writs authorizing the elections to be made out and issued. In every place entitled to be represented in Parliament is a person called "the Returning-Officer," whose duty is to manage the election. In counties the sheriff, and in cities and boroughs the mayor, bailiff, or some other person duly appointed, is the returning-officer. The writs are despatched to these returning-officers, commanding them to elect their members, which they must do in boroughs within six days after the receipt of the writ; while in counties twelve days are allowed, but the election must not be held sooner than the sixth day. Upon the day fixed, called the *nomination day*, a covered platform called the *hustings*, is erected in the principal town in counties, and in some convenient locality in other places, upon which the candidates for election and their friends assemble. The returning-officer takes the oath against bribery, and for the proper discharge of his duties. The candidates are *proposed* by one supporter, and *seconded* by another. They then address the electors, stating their political opinions and their claims to represent them. If the number of persons proposed does not exceed that which the electors are entitled to send to Parliament, they are elected then and there; if more be put in nomination, and a contest arises, the returning-officer calls for "a show of hands," and declares which candidate has the greatest number held up for him, but as there is no way of discovering whether all who thus give their vote are entitled to one, any candidate unwilling to abide by this decision, may demand a *poll*. When this is taken, each elector appears before persons appointed by the returning-officer as his deputies, and decides for which candidate he intends to vote. This vote is entered by the clerks in the *poll-books*, which, at the expiration of the time allowed by law for polling, are taken to the returning-officer. The votes are added up, and the candidates who are found to have gained the highest number are declared by him to be *duly elected*. In counties the poll remains open for two days, in cities and boroughs for one only. No "treating" whatever is permitted, nor are any bands of music and flag-bearers tolerated. In defiance of all these precautions, however, bribery and intimidation are by no means extinct. It is said that *the Ballot* (that is, secret voting, by placing a written paper in a box) would be a great protection to the electors. But I doubt whether it would remedy the evils complained of. I do not think it would prevent the corrupt from buying and selling votes. In large constituencies it matters little to a man how his vote is given as far as his business or trade is affected by it; there are plenty of his own way of thinking to support him. In small constituencies, where an adverse vote would deprive him of custom, it can be pretty easily gleaned from his habits and associations how he has decided, notwithstanding that the ballot does not betray him.

The Member of Parliament thus elected may be deprived of his seat, if it can be proved before a committee of the House of Commons that he, or his agents, with his knowledge, have been guilty of bribery, corruption, or undue influence in obtaining votes; or if it be found that persons had voted for him who had no right to do so, and that when their votes were deducted, his opponent had a majority of duly-qualified electors.

Should a vacancy occur during the sitting of Parliament, the Speaker, by order of the House, issues his warrant to the clerk of the Crown, and the writ is sent down, as I have narrated. If it happens during the recess, if the Speaker is informed of it in writing, signed by two members of Parliament, the writ is issued without an order of the House.

A member properly returned may be expelled the House for misconduct, and his seat will become vacated if he be made bankrupt, and does not satisfy his creditors within a year, or if he accepts an office under the Crown; he may, however, be re-elected, and afterwards fill it. A member may not resign the trust confided to him; but by his acceptance of the stewardship of the Chiltern Hundreds, or of the Manor of Northstead (sinecure offices under the Crown preserved for the purpose), his seat will be vacated and he can thus retire from Parliament. He cannot be made liable for anything that he may say in debate. The Lower House has the right to originate all bills relating to, or affecting the revenue and the taxation of the kingdom, and to vote the supplies; nor can any bills dealing with the taxation of the country be altered or amended by the House of Lords. That House can only reject them, or pass them in the form in which they come up from the Commons.

LETTER VI.

THE ADVISERS OF THE CROWN.

The Privy Council—The Judicial Committee — The Cabinet Council—The Attorney- and Solicitor-General—The Ministry, its Composition and Policy—The Opposition—Pensions of Ministers.

I HAVE told you that the advisers of the sovereign are responsible for his political acts; I must now tell you who these are.

The principal council of the crown is the Privy Council. Its members (whose number is now unlimited,) are appointed by the sovereign, and can be removed at her pleasure. The oath taken by a privy councillor upon entering office is as follows:

1. To advise the queen according to the best of his cunning and discretion.

2. To advise for the queen's honour and good of the public without partiality through affection, love. meed, doubt, or dread.

3. To keep the queen's counsel secret.

4. To avoid corruption.

5. To help and strengthen the execution of what shall be there resolved.

6. To withstand all persons who would attempt the contrary. And, lastly,

7. To observe, keep, and do all that a good and true counsellor ought to do to his sovereign lord.

The power of this Council as a body has of late years been very much diminished. Its *judicial* business (which mainly consists of hearing appeals from the courts in our *plantations* or colonies, and from the Admiralty and Ecclesiastical Courts) is transacted by a committee of judges and other eminent lawyers made members for the purpose; and its duties of advising the Crown and conducting the government of the country are almost exclusively performed by the principal ministers of State, who are members of the *Cabinet Council.* This is so termed on account of its being originally composed of such members of the Privy Council as the king placed most trust in, and conferred with apart from the others in his *cabinet* or private room. Curiously enough, although it is a body of the highest importance—being in fact the government of the country—it is not recognised in any way by the constitution. It is not, even in any strict or formal sense, a Committee of the Privy Council, to which however its members always belong.

The criminal jurisdiction of the Privy Council, that in the days of the Star Chamber (which was composed of its members), was stretched to so dangerous a length, is now no greater than that exercised by justices of the peace.

Her Majesty is frequently empowered by act of parliament to make proclamations and orders upon given subjects, " by and with the advice of her Privy Council," but only such members as are specially summoned attend upon each occasion.

Privy councillors are distinguished by having the words "*right honourable*" prefixed to their christian names or initials.

The sovereign may appoint her own ministry, or may order any person to form one; but as a majority in parliament is indispensable for the carrying on of government, it follows that, in *practice*, the ministry is composed of the leader of the political party in power, assisted by his friends and supporters. The Cabinet Council, shortly termed *the Cabinet*, forms only part of the ministry or *administration*. It usually consists of the following great officers of state:

The First Lord of the Treasury. This office is now generally filled by the *Premier*, or first minister, but he *may* hold any other.

The Lord High Chancellor—the law adviser of the ministry; and keeper of the great seal.

The Lord President of the Council.
The Postmaster-General.
The Lord Privy Seal.
The Secretary of State for Foreign Affairs—who conducts our intercourse with foreign nations.
The Secretary of State for the Colonies.
The Secretary of State for the Home Department—who manages the internal affairs of the kingdom.
The Secretary of State for the War Department.
The Secretary of State for India.
The Chancellor of the Exchequer—who arranges and accounts to Parliament for the public revenue and expenditure.
The Chancellor of the Duchy of Lancaster.
The First Lord of the Admiralty—who presides over the affairs of the Royal Navy.
The President of the Board of Trade—who attends to matters relating to trade and commerce.

Distinguished statesmen who hold no office under government are sometimes made members of the Cabinet.

Members of the Ministry must have seats either in the House of Lords or Commons.

Many other political offices subordinate to those I have mentioned, and a number of places in her Majesty's Household are filled by members of the party in power, who resign them when their friends go out of office.

The chief legal adviser of the Crown is the Lord Chancellor; its law officers are the Attorney- and Solicitor-General and Queen's Advocate. The two former are selected from amongst the most distinguished Queen's Counsel (a grade in the legal profession which I will explain in due course). They have to investigate the claims of inventors to *letters-patent*, by which the sole right to use or permit the use of the invention is secured to its owner for fourteen years. They represent the Crown in the courts of law and equity, the Attorney-General being in strictness entitled to a brief in every criminal prosecution, but only such as are of great difficulty and importance are undertaken by him. In cases of high treason both these officers invariably appear. The Queen's Advocate acts for the Crown in the Admiralty, and other courts where the civil law is administered.

A Ministry usually belongs to a distinct political party, and accepts office pledged to carry out some particular plan or policy of government. The party in Parliament that is opposed to this is called the *Opposition*. The Ministerial members—those who generally support the Ministry—sit on the right hand side of the Speaker's chair in the House of Commons, and those of the Opposition on the left. In the House of Lords—substituting the throne for the Speaker's chair—the same rule is generally observed, except upon high state occasions, when the Lords take their seats upon separate benches, according to the rank that they hold in the peerage, irrespective of their political opinions. When the Ministry is defeated—that is, placed in a minority upon some question intimately connected with the policy under which they took office; or if a vote of want of confidence is passed against them, they should resign, and, constitutionally speaking, the Opposition ought to be able to take their place.

When ministers have served for a period of three years, they are each entitled to a pension of £2000 for life on retirement; in computing which period it is usual to reckon the aggregate tenure of office, if it should happen that any of them have served more than once.

LETTER VII.

PROCEEDINGS IN PARLIAMENT.

Opening of Parliament—Election and Duties of Speaker—The Speech from the Throne—The Business of Government—Passing Bills, public and private—Divisions of the House—Voting by Peers,—by the Commons—The Royal Assent—The Budget—Committee of "Ways and Means"—Of Supply—Mutiny Act—Prorogation.

WHEN the day fixed for the meeting of a new parliament arrives, the members of both houses assemble and take the oaths prescribed by law. The Commons then, under an order from the crown, proceed to elect their speaker. The duty of this great officer is to regulate the debates in parliament, and to see that its proceedings are formally conducted. His decision upon any question of order is generally final, owing to the great respect which is paid to his high position, but an appeal against his judgment may be, and sometimes has been, made to the House. He does not vote except when there is an equal division. His salary is

6,000*l.* a year, with a house and allowances, and upon retirement he is usually created a peer.

When her Majesty opens parliament, she goes in state to the House of Lords, and takes her seat upon the throne. The Commons are then summoned, and such members as please attend, with their Speaker, at the bar. The royal speech, prepared beforehand by the Ministry, and in which the present condition of public affairs is briefly set forth, and the new measures to be submitted to the Legislature adverted to, is handed to the Queen by the Lord Chancellor and read by her; after which, her Majesty retiring, the business of the session commences. The Commons return to their own chamber, and, by way of form, read some bill to keep up their privilege of not giving priority to the royal speech. Two members appointed by government then move and second "the address" in either House, thanking her Majesty for her gracious speech, and each appoints a deputation to present it. In former days, the debate upon the address was often very vehemently contested, and "*amendments*" or alterations, implying a refusal to accept the intended policy of the Ministry, were frequently proposed; but of late, although the leaders of the Opposition in each House usually criticise closely the topics contained in, or omitted from, *the speech*, the address is generally passed without further opposition.

When Parliament is opened by Commission, the royal speech is read by one of the commissioners, and the address passed as I have stated.

The business of making and altering the laws is carried on by each House of Parliament, independently of the other. No proceeding which has taken place in the one may properly be alluded to in the other, nor may any past debate of the same session be mentioned. Their deliberations are supposed to be secret, and although the public is admitted to hear the debates, and reporters from the newspapers attend regularly to publish them, this is only practically permitted by a foolish fiction under which their presence is ignored. For should any member draw the attention of the Speaker to the fact, that there are strangers in the House, he has no alternative but to order them to withdraw. There are parts of the House to which strangers may be admitted when no objection is made, but any attempt to trespass upon the portion set apart for members of Parliament would be treated as a serious contempt. By a curious fiction, the space immediately around the Throne and the Woolsack, in the House of Lords, is deemed not to be a part of that House. So that when the Lord Chancellor wishes to speak, he moves from the Woolsack to the front of the head of the ducal bench, and from thence addresses the peers.

The only official report of proceedings in Parliament is printed by the Queen's printer.

I have already stated the measures which it is the privilege of the Lords or Commons to originate. There is one bill only which the Crown has the right of initiating—an Act of General Pardon. This is originated by the sovereign, and read *once* in each House of Parliament. All others may be introduced in either House, and by any member; only such as are of great public importance are generally taken charge of by the Government, who having certain days of the week exclusively devoted to the discussion of the bills they bring in, have better opportunities of passing them. Government bills are entrusted to the head of the department which conducts that branch of the administration which the proposed new law will affect. Thus, bills relating to the colonies are brought in by the Colonial Secretary; to police, prisons, &c., by the Home Secretary; to taxes, by the Chancellor of the Exchequer, &c. &c.

Bills are either public—relating to the general government of the kingdom; or private—such as

Estate, Railway, Dock, and Enclosure bills, which have only a local or personal operation.

The House of Lords meets at five o'clock in the afternoon, the House of Commons at four o'clock, except on Wednesdays, when it sits at noon. In both Houses, however, morning sittings are sometimes specially appointed. Before the commencement of business in either prayers are read; in the Lords by one of the bishops in turn, and in the Commons by the Speaker's chaplain. Three members must be present in the former, and forty in the latter, or there is what is called "*no house*," and business is adjourned until the next day.

In the House of Lords a peer merely gives notice of his intention to bring in a bill, but a member of the Lower House must obtain its leave to do so before he can introduce it. If permission be given, the bill, in manuscript, with blank spaces for dates, numbers, and other particulars likely to be altered, is brought in, and the introducer moves that it be read a first time. Every motion made in the Lower House must be seconded. In the House of Lords no seconder is required. When leave is given the bill is read a first time, and ordered to be printed; copies of it are distributed amongst the members, and upon the day fixed it is read a second time, and its *principle* then fully discussed, matters of detail being reserved for arrangement in the next stage, when the House goes into "committee" upon it. When this takes place, the Speaker quits the chair, and another parliamentary officer, *the chairman of committees*, presides. Each clause is read over in order, and altered, added to, improved, or struck out, as the majority decide, and sometimes the bill is entirely remodelled. In this stage a member may speak several times upon the same subject; at other times he may only speak once. When the bill has been gone through to the end in this manner, the Speaker resumes his place, and the chairman brings up the report of the committee, which is, in effect, the bill itself with its amendments. The House may then add improvements of its own, and accept or reject those made in committee. The bill is then engrossed upon parchment, and read a third time, and if agreed to, the question is put, "that the bill do pass," when it may be further altered. If this motion be carried, the bill is sent to the other House of Parliament, where it has to go through the same process over again. If it be amended there, it is sent back with the alterations made, to which, if the House which originated it agree, a message is sent to say so; if not, a conference between the two Houses takes place, and the difference between them is generally settled; but if this cannot be done, the bill is abandoned. On a bill passed by the Commons being sent up to the Lords, the clerk of the former endorses on it "*Soi ballé aux Seigners;*" and the same form is observed by the clerk of the Lords on a bill being sent to the Commons, the endorsement being "*Soi ballé aux Communes.*"

When the bill has passed through both Houses in this manner, it is ready to receive the royal assent, which is given either by her Majesty in person or by commission. When her Majesty gives her consent in person, her concurrence is previously communicated to the clerk-assistant, who reads the titles of the bills, on which the royal assent is signified by a gentle inclination. If it be a bill of supply, the clerk pronounces loudly, "*La reigne remercie ses bons sujets, accepte leur bénévolence, et ansi le veult.*" "The Queen thanks her good subjects, accepts their benevolence, and answers, 'Be it so.'" To other public bills the form of assent is "*La reigne le veult,*"—"The Queen wills it so." To private bills, "*Soi fait comme il est désiré,*" "Be it as it is prayed." When the royal assent is refused, the clerk says, "*La reigne s'avisera,*" "The Queen will consider of it;" but these words are never now pronounced, and have not been heard since Queen Anne refused to sanction the Scotch Militia Bill in the year 1707.

A bill may be opposed at any, or all, of its stages. When it is intended to do so, after a sufficient discussion has taken place, the "question" is "put" by the Speaker, and the House is *divided*. Those members who vote for the bill, or amendment in it, go into one lobby of the House, and those who vote against them into another. *Tellers*, or counters of the voters on either side, (generally the mover and seconder of the bill and two of its principal opponents), are appointed to ascertain the numbers in each. The result is written down upon a slip of paper, which is handed by the teller of the side that has a majority to the Speaker, who declares it to the House. The Speaker does not vote except when the House is equally divided, he then may give a casting vote. In "committee" he is entitled to speak and vote like any other member.

In the House of Lords, peers vote by the words "*content*" and "*non-content,*" and many use proxies, as already explained. In the Commons, members must be present, and signify their wish by saying "aye" or "no." If the "noes" are in a majority, the bill, or amendment, is lost; if the "ayes" prevail, the bill proceeds, or the amendment stands part of it. Bills must pass through all their stages in one session. So a formal method of throwing one out, is to move that it be read a second time "that day six months," when it is almost certain that Parliament will not be sitting. Bills are also sometimes referred to *select committees* chosen by the House in which they are introduced. These committees deliberate and examine witnesses, to ascertain whether the proposed measure is essential or otherwise, in apartments provided for the purpose, and report the result of their investigations to the House.

Private and personal bills may be introduced in either House of Parliament. They are based upon *petitions*, and if they propose to interfere with the land or property of any one, their purport must be advertised in the public papers. They are referred to a committee charged to investigate their provisions, before which persons interested in or affected by them may appear by counsel. The committee makes its report to the House, and they are passed or rejected in the same manner as public bills.

Early in the session the Chancellor of the Exchequer lays his *Budget* (from the French word *bougette*, a bundle) before Parliament. This contains an estimate of the sum required for the service of the State, for the Army, Navy, Civil Service, &c., &c., and the means proposed for raising it by taxation, or otherwise. The duration of a Ministry very often depends upon the correctness and sound financial policy of its Chancellor of the

Exchequer. The sum required is voted, or refused, in *Committee of Ways and Means*, and if granted, the manner in which it is to be applied is discussed, item by item, in *Committee of Supply*, in which members are at liberty to ask questions as to its application, which must be answered by the Minister to whose department they refer. The resolutions in Committee of Supply are embodied into what is called *the Appropriation Bill*, which is sent up for approval to the House of Lords. This House may reject, but cannot alter it.

To pass the Mutiny Act is also the annual business of Parliament. In former days the monarch often used the army to control the liberties of the subject. To remedy any abuse of power in this respect, it has for many years been the custom to pass the laws relating to the discipline and regulation of the army for one year only, to be renewed the next. If anything happened to prevent the Mutiny Act being passed in proper time, the whole of our army would be in fact disbanded.

When the business of the session is concluded, Parliament is *prorogued*, or, if necessary, dissolved, by the sovereign in person, or by commission, when a royal speech is delivered commenting upon the proceedings of the session, the state of public affairs, and thanking the Commons for voting the supplies.

LETTER VIII.

THE NATIONAL DEBT.

*Its Origin—The Funds—Funding System—Transfer of Stock—
Price of Money—Reduction of Debt—Sinking Fund—Amount
of Debt at various periods of our History—Revenue—Exports
and Imports—Balance of Trade.*

THE National Debt consists of sums borrowed by Government to make up deficiencies of revenue. Charles II. was the first king of Great Britain who borrowed money on the national credit; this began in 1660. At the abdication of James II., in 1688, the amount of the debt was 660,000*l*. But it was his successor who established the system. The Revolution, and the consequent banishment of the house of Stuart, involved us in a long and costly war with Louis XIV. of France, who espoused the cause of our exiled king. The seat of his son-in-law, William III., upon the vacated throne, was by no means secure. A large and powerful party of Englishmen still remained true to James II. as king *de jure* (*of right*), and many others only just tolerated the sway of the *de facto* sovereign. Money, far beyond what the ordinary revenue of the country would provide, was required to defray the heavy expenses of the struggle which we were compelled to wage, in defence of our religion and liberties; and it was felt that it would be dangerous in the extreme to impose new taxes sufficient to meet the demand.

The cause of Louis was the cause of James, and it was not to be expected that the adherents of the latter would quietly submit to heavy imposts designed to furnish means for destroying their fondest hopes. It was, therefore, determined to borrow money upon interest, and to repay it when the resources of the country were in a more flourishing condition. But the exigencies of the public service went on increasing, and loan after loan was contracted. Other wars were engaged in—again the national expenditure became greater than its income, and ministry after ministry added to the debt, until not only do we find it existing at the present day, but (notwithstanding that large portions of it have been paid off from time to time), existing to the enormous extent of *eight hundred millions of pounds!* besides sums due upon *Exchequer bills* (promissory notes issued by Government for temporary purposes) which constitute the *unfunded debt.*

The term *fund* applied originally to the taxes or funds set apart, as security, for repayment of the principal sums advanced and the interest upon them; but when money was no longer borrowed to be repaid at any given time, it began to mean the principal sum itself. In the year 1751, Government began to unite the various loans into one fund, called the *Consolidated fund* (which you must not confuse with that of the same name into which part of the revenue is collected), and sums due in this are now shortly termed *consols*. These come under the general denomination of *stocks*.

The interest paid upon loans during the reigns of William III. and Anne was various; but latterly, instead of varying the interest upon the loan, according to the state of the money-market at the time, it was fixed at three and a half per cent., the necessary addition being made in the principal funded. Thus, suppose that Government could not borrow money under four and a half per cent., they would give the lender 150*l*. three per cent. stock for every 100*l*. he advanced, and the country would be bound to pay him 4*l*. 10*s*. a year as interest until the debt was extinguished by a payment of 150*l*. This was eventually found to be a very bad plan, and it was calculated, when it was discontinued, that owing to its adoption, the debt then existing amounted to nearly two-fifths more than the sum actually advanced, and that we were paying from 6,000,000*l.* to 7,000,000*l.* a year in interest more than would have been due had the money been borrowed at the market rate of the day, and funded without increase of capital. For the market rate of interest might fall the week after the loan was contracted, whereas the additional capital funded remained undiminished.

A portion of the revenue is set apart every year to pay the interest upon the national debt to such persons as have themselves lent money, and to those by whom the claims of others have been inherited, or to whom they have been transferred. The person to whom stock is transferred need not receive any certificate of the transfer, but his name is registered in the national debt books. If he disposes of the whole or any part of it, this is again transferred from his name to that of its new proprietor. The registry books are arranged alphabetically in the Bank of England, and distributed in several apartments, marked with the initial letter and syllables of the book they contain. Thus everybody is able to find the exact place where his account is kept. The business of buying and selling stock, however, is almost entirely in the hands of the *stock-brokers*, who become agents for the parties who wish to procure or part with it, and transact all the necessary operations upon their behalf. The Bank of England manages the payment of interest upon the funds for Government.

The sum required in the year 1865 to pay the interest upon the funded and unfunded debt is 26,350,000*l.*

The value of a nominal 100*l.* of stock fluctuates according to the abundance or scarcity of money in circulation. During the last hundred years the market price of 100*l.* in the 3 per cent. consols has been as low as $47\frac{1}{4}$, and as high as $101\frac{1}{4}$. Anything that tends to endanger or lessen the national prosperity causes the Funds to sink, and *vice versâ*. Foreign nations have attempted to keep up the price of their stocks by force of law, but have failed signally. Money, like water, will find its own level, and no legislative enactments will cause any permanent increase, or the contrary, in its value.

I saw that you were much puzzled once when your uncle and I were talking of the *price of money*. You thought, no doubt, that sovereigns and shillings were of a fixed and unalterable value; and as far as regards their shape and weight they are so. But really and practically they are no more than pieces of gold and silver, worth just as much as you can get in exchange for them, and no more. A sovereign represents so much land or so many legs of mutton, or pieces of ribbon, or cricket-bats, or anything else that we may require. If there are only a very few legs of mutton in the market, and plenty of sovereigns to buy them with, the holders of money must (*practically*) compete with all other persons requiring meat, and give as much for it as any of them will pay. If, on the other hand, legs of mutton are numerous, and there are very few sovereigns in circulation, the tables are turned—the butcher must compete (in the same way as before) for the money, and give as much meat as others will in return for the gold. Therefore, when you say that certain things are *cheap* or *dear*, you mean, in other words, that they are plentiful or the reverse.

For the gradual reduction of the principal of the national debt, *sinking funds* were established; the first by Sir Robert Walpole in the year 1716, the second by Mr. Pitt in 1786. By the latter an estimated surplus of 900,000*l.* in the revenue was augmented by taxes, so as to make up a sum of one million; and this was to be applied every year towards paying off the public creditors. As long as this, or *any* surplus remained over expenditure, it might be properly and successfully applied to this purpose; the time came, however, when there was no such thing, but the sinking fund did not disappear with it. We were soon at war again, and obliged to make new loans to supply a *deficiency*, but the 900,000*l.* was still applied as before, and the fund still deserved (in one sense) the term by which it was known, for it was sinking the nation deeper and deeper in debt. We were discharging liabilities upon which a small amount of interest was due with one hand, and contracting fresh ones upon which we had to pay a large interest with the other. We were, in fact, following the example of the Irishman in the story, who, finding that his blanket was not long enough to cover the upper part of his bed, cut a piece off its other end to supply the deficiency! The financiers of the day were deluded by a fascinating theory that the sinking fund accumulating upon *compound interest* (that is, interest upon interest) would in time equal the debt. Dr. Price, at whose instigation the second sinking fund was established, attempted to prove this by calculating how many *globes of gold* a penny invested at compound interest at the birth of Jesus Christ, would amount to at the date of his investigation. But to secure the marvellous increase effected in time by compound interest, all the proceeds must be re-invested and added to the capital, not expended as income; and this was never actually done. Experience proved that the system was a fallacious one, and it was discontinued. Now nothing but actual excess of revenue over expenditure is applied for the reduction of the National Debt.

One of the methods successfully adopted for decreasing the amount of interest paid upon the funds, was for Government to offer—when it had a surplus in hand—to redeem sums of stock unless the holders agreed to accept a lower rate upon them; and as this was proposed at the market price of the day, they were frequently willing to do so.

Most other nations have contracted public debts, but the National Debt of England exceeds the heaviest known; and this fact is often thrown in our teeth, when the greatness of our country is the subject of discussion. But, such is the vastness of our trade and the elasticity of our resources, that the impost is by no means insupportable. Indeed some maintain that we are better off with it, than we should be without it. I do not go so far as this. The debt, however, is the price we pay for the position (out of all proportion to their geographical limits) which these little islands have won. Some of the wars, for carrying on which it was incurred, might have been averted probably, or brought to speedier termination; but others were most necessary, and, taking the rough with the smooth, it is very fair that posterity should bear a portion of the burden, as they participate in the experiences and benefits it secured.

The following table will show you the amount of the National Debt (both funded and unfunded) at various periods of our history down to the year 1864 :—

YEAR.	OCCASION.	AMOUNT.
1688.	On the accession of William III.	£660,000
1702.	On the accession of Queen Anne	16,500,000
1714.	On the accession of George I.	54,000,000
1749.	At the end of the Spanish war	78,000,000
1763.	At the end of the Seven Years' war	139,000,000
1786.	Three years after the American war	268,000,000
1798.	After the Irish rebellion and foreign war	462,000,000
1802.	Close of the French revolutionary war	571,000,000
1814.	Close of the war against Buonaparte	865,000,000
1817.	When the English and Irish Exchequers were consolidated	840,850,491
1850.		790,927,016
1856.	Conclusion of the war with Russia	803,913,694
1860.		802,190,300
1864.		790,565,224

Our average revenue during the reign of William III. was about 4,000,000*l.*; in that of George I. it was 6,000,000*l.*; in that of George II., 8,000,000*l.*; in the year 1788, it had risen to 15,572,971*l.* In 1820 the sum raised by taxes in the United Kingdom was 65,599,570*l.*; in 1825 it fell to 62,871,300*l.*; in 1830 it was 55,431,317*l.*; in 1835 it was 50,494,732*l.*; in 1845 it was 51,067,856*l.*; in 1850 it was 52,951,748*l.*; in 1855, during the Russian war, it was 84,505,788*l.*; and in the year 1864, 70,313,000*l.*

To show you the wealth of our country, the declared value of our *exports* was—

In 1853 ... £99,000,000
„ 1855 ... 95,000,000 (year of war.)
„ 1856 ... 116,000,000
„ 1857 ... 122,000,000
„ 1864 ... 213,000,000

Our imports were—

In 1853 ... £123,099,313
„ 1854 ... 124,338,478
„ 1855 ... 143,000,000
„ 1856 ... 172,000,000
„ 1857 ... 187,000,000
„ 1864 ... 274,000,000

With regard to the disparity in value which exists between our exports and our imports, I may observe that it used to be urged that this showed an unsound state of commerce. The *balance of trade*, it was said, was against us, as we *took* more from foreign nations than we *gave*. I can show you the fallacy of this argument by a very simple illustration. Suppose a merchant were to send to America (for example) 1,000*l.* worth of goods, and selling them at a profit, ship homeward a cargo of the value of 1,500*l.* If this arrives safely his imports exceed his exports, and (according to the above theory) he is rapidly becoming bankrupt; but if they all sink to the bottom of the sea and are lost, then he is a most flourishing trader Exports are the *price* of imports, and (as gold is now reckoned in the category of both as an article of commerce), it is quite clear that if we buy more than we sell it must be because we are selling at a profit.

LETTER IX.

LOCAL GOVERNMENT.

Its Principle, Origin, and Objects—High Sheriff and Lord Lieutenant of the County—Local Rates—The Parish and its Officers—The Constable—Churchwardens—Surveyor of Highways—The Vestry, General and Select—The Poor Law—The Law of Settlement—Operation of the old Poor Law—The new Poor Law—Municipal Corporations—Town Councils—Mayor and Aldermen—Boards of Health—Improvement Commissioners.

You now know how the general government of the kingdom is carried on. I purpose, in this Letter, to show you how the affairs of the counties, cities, boroughs, and parishes of which it is composed are regulated.

It is a fundamental principle of the British Constitution, that all persons and communities shall be allowed to manage their own affairs as long as they do so regularly and according to law. For it is only natural to conclude, that those whose comfort and welfare are to be considered, who will be the first and principal sufferers by neglectful or bad government, are much more likely to know what ought to be done than strangers, however well intentioned they may be, who have not the same knowledge and experience. The powers of local governments are fixed by the common law, by charter from the Crown, and by act of Parliament.

The most ancient division of the country for the purpose of self-government was into shires, hundreds, and tithings. At present the usual divisions are counties, hundreds, boroughs, and parishes. The ministerial and judicial business of the county is transacted by the High Sheriff, the Coroner, and the Justices of the Peace, and is enforced in it by the former and his officers. Its military government is confided to the Lord Lieutenant, who, when occasion requires, with the aid of his Deputy Lieutenants, calls out the Militia, of which force he has the command; and the commissions of all its officers, with the exceptions which I shall state hereafter, are signed by him. He is frequently the *custos rotulorum*, or keeper of the records of the county, and attends the Sovereign when he passes through it. The post of Lord Lieutenant in counties was instituted in England by Edward III., in the year 1549, and extended to Ireland in 1831. The appointment, which is a purely honorary one, is made by the Crown, and is for life.

The office of Sheriff is of much greater antiquity. His office is of Saxon origin, and its name is derived from the words *shire gerefa,* or *shire reeve.* He was inferior to the Earl only when that was the title of the county's military governor, and is now the chief man in it as his successor.

Sheriffs hold office for one year only. The Lord Lieutenant prepares a list of persons qualified to serve, and returns three names, which are read out in the Court of Exchequer upon the morrow of the Feast of St. Martin, when the excuses of such as do not wish to serve are heard, and if deemed sufficient, the objector is discharged. The list is then sent to the Sovereign, who, without looking at it, strikes a bodkin amongst the names, and he whose name is pierced is elected. This is called *"pricking for sheriffs."* The duty of the High Sheriff being chiefly to execute the law, will be treated of by-and-bye. The affairs of the boroughs are administered by the municipal corporations, and of the parishes by the constable, churchwardens, and surveyor of highways, and, where there is one, the *vestry.*

The principal objects of local government are the preservation of peace and order; the maintenance of the poor and police; the making, paving, and lighting of roads and streets; the repairing of bridges; the regulation of markets, hackney coaches, and public carriages; the laying down of rules for preserving the public health and convenience, &c. The money required for these purposes is raised by levying *rates*. Every person who is not exempted by extreme poverty, or some privileges which I need not particularize, is *rated* according to the value of the premises which he occupies. The sum required for the rate is estimated, and each liable person is called upon to pay his portion; when you hear, therefore, of a poor, or any other rate of one shilling in the pound, it means that for every pound at which a person is rated, according to the value of his house or property, he has to pay that sum.

I shall tell you hereafter how justices of the peace are appointed. They lay the county rates for maintaining the police, &c. &c. The Lord Lieutenant and his deputies regulate the county militia.

The constitution of *parishes* and *municipal corporations* must now be considered.

The *constable** was formerly the chief man in

---

* "The next officer mentioned, after the sheriff, in Magna Charta, (c. 24) is *constabularius*, or *constable*, which is sometimes derived from the Saxon, but other authorities have considered it more truly to come from the Latin *comes stabuli*, a superinten-

the parish, for it was responsible for all robberies committed within its limits if the thieves were not apprehended. It was, therefore, the interest of the community to elect to this office the person who was most competent to prevent the commission of crime. But this state of things has long passed away; the parish may no longer be called upon to restore the value of stolen goods; and although constables are still appointed, their duties are almost entirely performed by the county police.

When the religion of this country was Roman Catholic, costly ornaments, and very often large sums of money, were kept in the parish churches, and men of character were therefore required to take charge of them, and to stand between the ignorant country people and their clergy, who monopolised all the learning of that time, and

---

dent of the imperial stables, or master of the horse. This title, however, began in the course of time to signify a commander, in which sense it was introduced into England. In the clause of Magna Charta referred to, the word is put for the constable, or keeper of a castle, frequently called a castellan: indeed, the term is still used occasionally in this sense in England, the governor of the Tower of London being styled *Constable of the Tower*. They were possessed of such considerable power within their own precincts, that previously to the Act of Magna Charta, they held trials of crimes, properly the cognisance of the Crown, as the sheriffs did within their respective bailiwicks; and sealed with their own effigies on horseback."—*Creasy's Rise and Progress of the English Constitution.*

often sought to encroach upon the rights of their fellow-subjects. *Churchwardens* were therefore appointed by the Synod of London in the year 1127, and continue to this day to be elected, to see that the parson does his duty, and to exercise authority over the building of the church, and the performance of its services. Two churchwardens are generally appointed annually, the one by the rector, vicar, or incumbent, the other by the parishioners.

The parish is bound to maintain the highways which pass through it in good order, and for this purpose *surveyors of highways*, or, as they were anciently called, *waywardens*, are elected by the parishioners and hold office for one year. Under a recent Act a number of parishes may be united into a highway district, the roads in which are managed by a board.

A *vestry* is a body of the ratepayers of a parish elected to conduct and regulate its business, including the appointment of its officers. When it is elected by the ratepayers at large it is called a *general* vestry; if (as is more frequently the case), its members select their own companions and successors, it is called a *select* vestry.

The maintenance of its poor is the most important duty of the parish, and as this is a subject upon which you ought to be informed, I will give you a brief sketch of the origin and progress of the laws relating to it.

Previously to the dissolution of the monasteries, the maintenance and relief of the poor were secured by the great religious houses: their endowments being required, in most cases, by the charters of foundation, and in all, by the statute of Carlisle (Ed. I. A.D. 1306), to be expended to the honour of God and in support of His poor. When these institutions were suppressed, and their property distributed among the monarch's courtiers, the helpless and indigent, the aged and the young, were at once deprived of all provision. The greedy rapacity of the king's attendants, and the absorbing controversies of religion, were not favourable to the discovery or the adoption of any substitute for the funds so disposed of. All that the authorities of that time devised were severe and stringent measures directed against the numerous mendicants by whom the country began to be infested. Vagrancy and begging were made punishable by whipping, the stocks, the pillory, imprisonment, and death; and the executions of "sturdy beggars," as they were termed, increased year by year until, in the last years of Henry VIII.'s reign, no fewer than 38,000 persons were put to death for this species of offence! The same repressive system followed under the subsequent sovereigns, until the power of Queen Elisabeth having been firmly established towards the latter part of her reign, the foundations of a new system were laid. This was done by an act passed in the 43rd year of that queen. Its principal provisions were, that a fund or stock should be raised in each parish, out of which such poor persons as were able to labour should be set to work, and the feeble should be helped and maintained. The churchwardens were appointed, together with three or four more persons of substance, *overseers of the poor*. The operation of the statute was found beneficial; and the lawlessness and violence, which had not been suppressed by barbarous enactments, disappeared by degrees. Gradually an entirely new code of legislation arose, as experience developed the benefits and the disadvantages of the system; and its ramifications embraced, as well the support of the indigent, as the adjustment of the liabilities of the contributors. Thus, in the time of Charles II. the parish, which had enjoyed the benefit of a man's residence as a contributor to the parish rates, or as a labourer when he was able to support himself, was bound to maintain him when in distress, in preference to that where he might become in want.

Hence arose what is called *the law of settlement*. The contribution itself was called the poor-rate, and the contributors ratepayers. The ratepayers had not the power of electing the overseers of the poor directly, these officers being nominated by justices of the peace. In many parishes the overseers of the poor were assisted, and sometimes controlled, by a select vestry.

In the course of nearly three centuries some abuses of greater or less magnitude could not but be expected to grow around the system. The chief source of these was alleged to arise from the administrators of the rate being appointed by others than the ratepayers, and the great evil apprehended was that a class of persons receiving relief, habitually and as the ordinary rule, were growing up under this system, and that to be a *pauper* (as the receivers of relief are called), was becoming a recognised and actual condition, or state, in the ranks of social life.

This general feeling, assisted by many matters of minor character, led to the enactment in the 5th and 6th years of William IV., of what is called a *test* for pauperism (a somewhat different thing from poverty, but which may be described as that state of destitution requiring to be relieved out of the poor-rate), by requiring that no relief

THE NEW POOR LAW. 77

should be given to any person whatever, except in the workhouse; but as many of the parishes in this country are so small as not to need or possess a workhouse, in order to apply this test several parishes were by the act joined together for the purpose of supporting such an establishment in common. These parishes thus joined together were called *Unions,* and for their government, and for the performance of a great number, but not all, of the powers of the overseers of the poor, a number of persons, called *Guardians of the Poor,* were constituted a Board. These are elected by the ratepayers annually in each parish of the Union. In order to obviate the recurrence of the old abuses, to ensure uniformity of administration, and to carry out the new test in its integrity, it was considered desirable to have a permanent establishment, called the Poor-Law Board, of which the President is usually a member of the Privy Council, and must possess a seat in the House of Commons.

The experience of a quarter of a century has modified the rigorous theory of the Amendment Act, and now a plan of administering relief in two modes—inside the workhouse and at the residence of the pauper (called out-door relief), is permitted.

It may be added, that the legislature has provided remedies for a parish or union which may consider itself aggrieved, and for a ratepayer in the same position. This is by the legal process called "an appeal," whereby if an union be called upon to maintain a pauper not belonging to it, or a parishioner is required to pay out of proportion to his neighbours, or for improper charges, the interference of the Court of Quarter Sessions is invoked. Against improper charges an additional remedy is provided by the appointment of an officer called a "Poor-Law Auditor," whose duty it is to check every account in connexion with the poor-rate and its expenditure, and who has power to disallow any item not justified by law.

I now come to the *Municipal Corporations*. In the year 1833, a royal commission was appointed to inquire into their state, and it being reported that they had degenerated into great inefficiency and corruption, an Act of Parliament was passed, by which most of the then existing Corporations were dissolved, and replaced by a municipal body consisting of mayor, aldermen, and burgesses. This law is known as the "Municipal Corporations Act."

All persons of full age, who have occupied for three years a house or shop within the limits of the borough to be incorporated, and those who have regularly resided within seven miles of its limits, and have during that time been rated to the relief of the poor of some parish in the borough, are entitled to be placed on the list of burgesses. The borough is divided into *wards*, or districts, and by the burgesses in every ward the *Common Councillors* are elected. The number of councillors is fixed by the Act for each borough, and one-third of them go out of office every year. The councillors elect *Aldermen*, whose number is one-third of their own. Thus is formed the *Town Council*, which elects the *Mayor*, whose business it is to preside over it. He holds office for only one year, but may be re-elected. Half the aldermen go out of office every third year, but may be re-elected. The town-council lay the borough rates.

In many populous towns not incorporated, *commissioners* and *boards*, such as *Boards of Health*, *Improvement Commissioners*, &c., &c., are elected by the ratepayers, under the authority of Parliament, to conduct useful works, and to manage the local business.

LETTER X.

THE CHURCH.

History of the Church of England—Authority of the Pope—The Reformation—Puritans—Roman Catholics—Jews, disabilities of—Constitution and Discipline of the Church—Bishop—Dean and Chapter—Priest—Deacon—Tithes—Ordinations—Church Accommodation—Convocation.

IN order to give you a right understanding of the relations of the ecclesiastical system and the Constitution of this country, it will be necessary briefly to sketch the history of the Church in England.

It is an undoubted fact that Christianity was very early introduced into this country whilst it was in the hands of the Romans, and tradition points to the numerous old churches dedicated to St. Paul, as a confirmation of the assertion that he was the apostle of Britain. However this may be, certain it is that in the third century numerous Christian congregations existed here, and the older chroniclers declare with a fond pride that Britain produced the first Christian emperor (Constantine the Great), the first Christian king (Lucius), and the first Christian monastery, that of Bangor in Wales. The Saxons, being idolatrous and exterminators, persecuted the native believers and drove them into the Welsh mountains. There they were found when Pope Gregory the Great sent hither the monk Augustine and his companions, on the occasion of the conversion of Ethelbert, King of Kent. Before this time the British Church was governed by its own bishops, but Augustine (by coercion as well as persuasion) induced the scattered bodies of the faithful to acknowledge his authority as *primate*, whilst he himself admitted the superiority of the Roman pontiff. Augustine, upon being consecrated Archbishop of Canterbury, received a present of a *pall* from the pope, and each of his successors applied for and obtained a like mark of distinction for many years after from succeeding occupants of the Papal chair, until it was asserted that an Archbishop of Canterbury could not enter upon his functions unless and until it was granted. This "pall" is an ecclesiastical vestment somewhat resembling in shape the hood now worn by clergymen to indicate the university degree of the wearer, and a symbol of it is still retained in the emblasonment of the arms of the province of Canterbury. Under the Norman kings, and the early Plantagenets, the claim to present this pall, and the rights which it was supposed to confer, were stoutly resisted. But what Henry II. refused to Thomas a'Beckett was conceded by his son John, who, as you know, humiliated himself so far as to hold his very crown as a *fief* under the pope. Notwithstanding the famous statute of *præmunire*, passed in the reign of Richard II., which is still unrepealed, and which I shall have occasion to mention again, the general results of various compromises made between different monarchs and popes amounted to this:—That, whilst in matters of faith and (to some extent) of discipline also, the Church of England gave obedience to Rome, in matters connected with the choice of bishops and the enjoyment of temporalities the royal supremacy was admitted.

The first stage of the Reformation in the reign of Henry VIII. was not made in reference to doctrine. The right of appeal from the English courts to the pope was that against which the king's policy was directed in the beginning, and the operation of the statute 25th Henry VIII. chapter 20, was to establish the jurisdiction of the Crown, and the king's tribunals, in entire independence of any foreign potentate. The words of what is called the *bidding prayer* (still used in cathedrals and other churches before sermon) indicate clearly the intention of the Constitution upon this point. It runs as follows: "Ye shall pray for all Christian kings, &c., and specially for our Sovereign Lady Queen Victoria, defender of the Faith, *over all persons, and in all causes ecclesiastical and civil, within these her dominions supreme.*" It is in this sense that the sovereign is called "the supreme head of the Church."

The policy of Elisabeth and of the Stuarts was to establish the Church of which they were members as the sole and exclusive form of religion. Hence non-attendance at a man's parish church, and non-conformity to its ordinances, were made by Convocation—of which I shall treat hereafter— the subject of spiritual censure, and by Parliament, of civil penalties, even of *death*. The theory of the Church down to so late a period as the reign of George IV., according to the Constitution, was that of an ecclesiastical corporation co-extensive with the State, every English subject being also an English churchman, and the Church a body absolutely *national*. Two great religious sections maintained a constant and, eventually, successful struggle against this theory,—I mean the Puritans and the Roman Catholics. The former party resorted to arms, and their victory in the contest against Archbishop Laud and his sovereign displaced for twelve years both the Church and her royal head. On the restoration of Charles II. the former doctrine was revived; and it was not until the accession of William III. that the *act of toleration*, permitting Protestants to meet to celebrate divine service after other forms than the liturgy—and in other places than the temples—of the Church of England was passed. More than a century and a half elapsed before persons who did not conform to the religion established by law were allowed to enter Parliament, and to take office in municipal corporations. Every man elected to either was obliged to partake of the holy sacrament, according to the rites and doctrine of the Church of England, as a *test*. It was not until the year 1828 that the statutes imposing this test were repealed. Thus terminated the contest with the first religious section I named. The result was that there was no longer a Constitution exclusively *Church of England*, but only necessarily *Protestant*. The following year saw the final success of the Roman Catholic body. Like the Protestant Dissenters, they had obtained various instalments of toleration. The objection to admit them to full rights of citizenship was based rather upon political than theological grounds, and they endured for many years the most vexatious disabilities intended to prevent their gaining wealth and influence, before it was discovered that being a papist did not prevent a man from also being an honest and a loyal subject. The Roman Catholic Relief Act, passed in the year 1829, placed Roman Catholics upon the same footing with their Protestant fellow-countrymen. Until 1858 British subjects professing the Jewish religion were excluded from senatorial rights and honours, not by any direct enactment of the legislature, but because the wording of the oath of supremacy, which had to be taken by all members of Parliament, prevented them from subscribing it; concluding, as it did, in the words, "*upon the true faith of a Christian.*" This form of words was adopted when this oath was framed, to prevent the jesuit adherents of the Pretender from swearing fealty to the king *de facto* with a mental reservation, but indirectly it had the effect I have stated. Our Jewish fellow-subjects could be judges, sheriffs, and magistrates. They could be called upon to carry the laws into execution, but had no part in framing them; they had to pay taxes, but had no voice in imposing them. They might vote at elections for others; nay, more!—they could be elected themselves, but could not take their seats. They might write M.P. after their names, but the doors of the Parliament house were firmly closed against them.

At last, however, after considerable opposition from the House of Lords, the excluding oath has been modified so as to admit the Jews to Legislative honours; and now the necessity for any religious profession whatever, as a condition for becoming a member of Parliament, is no longer in existence.

Thus the Church of England gradually ceased to be what at one time she was, and what many statesmen consider she ought to have remained— an integral and indivisible part of the Constitution. But although she has no longer the ancient prerogatives and high privileges that once were hers, she still occupies a position, and exercises an influence it is impossible to overlook, in a recapitulation such as I wish to make. Her antiquity and associations, her wealth and dignity, her venerable and majestic ritual, the learning and courageous exertions of her clergy, preserve for her respect and reverence, and are the legitimate foundations upon which the authority and power she exercises (independently of secular enactments) are substantially based. A short account, therefore, of the ecclesiastical system of the Church of England, as it now exists, cannot properly be omitted.

The whole of England and Wales is divided for church purposes into two *provinces*, Canterbury and York. The former is governed by its Archbishop and his *suffragans*, or inferior prelates, who are the Bishops of London, Winchester, Bangor, Bath and Wells, Bristol and Gloucester, Chichester, Ely, Exeter, Hereford, Llandaff, Lichfield and Coventry, Lincoln, Norwich, Oxford, Peterborough, Rochester, Salisbury, St. Asaph, St. David's, and Worcester. The province of York is governed by its Archbishop, and the Bishops of Durham, Carlisle, Chester, Manchester, Ripon, and Sodor and Man are his suffragans. In addition to his province and the appellate jurisdiction connected therewith, each Archbishop has a particular district within which he exercises original authority. The district over which a suffragan bishop presides is called his *diocese*, or *see* (from the Latin word for a *seat* or *chair*); and the principal church of his diocese is called the *cathedral* (from the Greek word of the same import), because it contains the episcopal *seat* or *throne*. The title *bishop* is derived from the Greek *episkopos*, through the Saxon *biscop*, both signifying an overseer, or superintendent, "so called from that watchfulness and faithfulness which by his place and dignity he hath and oweth to the church." Formerly bishops were elected by the clergy and people, but now the right to appoint them is in the crown. The form of an election by the chapter of the diocese is still preserved. When a vacancy occurs the Sovereign sends a permission to them to elect (called a *congé d'élire*), together with a *letter missive*, recommending the person therein named. Obedience to this recommendation is secured by the famous statute of *præmunire*, and some acts of Henry VIII., which direct, upon any delay or refusal, a forfeiture of all the real and personal property of the recusant parties with imprisonment at the king's pleasure, and other penalties. We have seen that a bishop is a peer of Parliament and sits in the House of Lords.

To assist the bishop in the government of his diocese generally, there are the *dean* and an indefinite number of *canons* or *prebendaries*, who form the *chapter*. It was once the duty of this body to educate candidates for holy orders, but they have ceased to do this. Indeed, the labours they perform are not of a very onerous character, although the fact of their being made a corporation, and the dean, their chief, sometimes a corporation sole, shows that at one time they must have discharged very high and important functions. The title *dean* is from the Latin word for *ten*, that being the usual number of canons or prebendaries in the early chapters. Sometimes there are on the cathedral foundation *minor canons*, and always *precentors, lay vicars*, and *choristers*. Occasionally grammar and singing schools are attached.

The country parts of the diocese not otherwise governed as above, are subdivided into archdeaconries and rural deaneries. By the Canon Law the archdeacon is called "the bishop's eye," and has power to hold visitations within his jurisdiction when the bishop is not present, to make institutions and inductions of benefices, to assist at the examination of candidates for orders, and also to enquire into, correct, and reform irregularities and abuses amongst the parochial clergy. The *rural dean* governs part of an archdeaconry, usually consisting of about ten parishes, and exercises a similar but more restricted authority over them. Finally, we have the parochial clergy, consisting of *rectors, vicars, incumbents,* and *curates.* The two former are usually distinguished as *beneficed clergy,* in contradistinction to the curates, who are assistants to them, acting under a licence from the bishop, which is revocable at his pleasure. The word "curate" signifies a person having the *cure* (or care) of souls. "Rector" is one who has the chief *rule* of the parish in ecclesiastical matters. The rector is entitled to the whole of the tithes of his parish (now commuted into a fixed annual sum called a *rent charge*). The vicar has only the *small* tithes. "Vicar" means a *substitute.* When, in days long passed away, the great landholders granted a rectory to a monastery, the living never became vacant, as the abbey or convent was a corporation, and corporations never die, although those who constitute them do. The monastery, as rector, took all the tithes, and sent a clergyman to perform divine service, to whom were given the small tithes as his recompence. By degrees the substitute thus sent acquired a permanent right to the benefice. When Henry VIII. confiscated to the crown the possessions of the religious houses, it was thought that their great tithes would revert to the vicar. This, however, was not agreeable to the grasping courtiers to whom the monarch had granted the property and estates, and an act of Parliament was, therefore, passed, which annexed the great tithes to the confiscated lands. Thus the position of the vicars remained unaltered.

An incumbent differs from a curate in being free from the liability to summary dismissal mentioned just now, as his ordinary title of *perpetual curate* shows; but he has no independent rule, and is in the eye of the law (notwithstanding his having sole authority in his own church), only an assistant to the rector or vicar of the parish in which it is situated.

It only remains for me now to tell you how a person is made a clergyman. It is the peculiar prerogative of the bishop alone to confer holy orders, which in our church are of three kinds—

those, namely, of bishop, priest, and deacon. When a layman is made a deacon he must be at least twenty-three years old, and (if not possessed of a university degree), a *"literate person"*—that is, one of competent learning and good education. The ceremony of making deacons is called ordination. After twelve months the deacon may be ordained a priest. A bishop must be a priest of at least thirty years of age, and is set apart for his office by three other bishops. This is called his *consecration*. The archdeacons (who are priests appointed to that office by the bishop) assist the bishop in ordinations. He has also his *examining chaplains* to aid him in testing the abilities of the candidates, who must each have a *title for orders*—that is, a sphere of labour under some clergyman, with a proper stipend for his support, before he can be ordained.

There are many matters which it is difficult to avoid touching upon in connexion with the subject of this letter, but which, if fully entered into, would swell it into the bulk of an entire volume. I will, in conclusion, refer to one which (especially in late times), has attained a degree of prominence that may have an important bearing upon the constitution—I mean the ecclesiastical parliament, called *Convocation*. This is an assembly of the spiritual estates of the realm in both provinces. In each it consists of an Upper and Lower House. In the former sit the bishops, presided over by the Archbishop as *Primate and Metropolitan*. The latter is composed of *Proctors* or delegates chosen by the chapters of cathedrals and the beneficed clergy. The members elect their own *Prolocutor* or Speaker. Formerly convocation granted to the Crown the right to tax the clergy. That usage has now ceased, and with it the state necessity for convoking the assembly yearly. Recently, however, ecclesiastical and spiritual necessities have caused its sittings to be in some degree available in a practical sense.

I shall conclude by giving you a table of the church accommodation provided by several of the religious denominations in England, published in the year 1855.

Religious Denomination.	No. of Places of Worship.	Sittings for
Church of England	14,077	5,317,915
Scottish Presbyterians:		
Church of Scotland	18	13,989
United Presbyterian Church	66	31,351
Presbyterian Church in England	76	41,552
Independents	3,224	1,067,760
Baptists (all denominations of)	3,789	752,253
Society of Friends	331	91,599
Unitarians	229	68,554
Moravians	32	9,305

CHURCH ACCOMMODATION.

Religious Denomination.	No. of Places of Worship.	Sittings for
Wesleyan Methodists:		
Original Connexion	6,596	1,447,580
New Connexion	297	96,964
Primitive Methodists	2,871	414,030
Independent Methodists	20	2,263
Bible Christians	482	66,834
Lutherans	6	2,606
Roman Catholics	570	186,111
Greek Church	3	291
Jews	53	8,438
Latter-Day Saints	222	30,783

Although the information contained in this table is now ten years old, it is the latest we possess in reference to the numbers of the different denominations; for in consequence of the opposition of the Dissenters the Government were compelled to abandon their intention of including in the census of 1861 returns relating to the religion of the people.

LETTER XI.

THE ARMY.

Origin and History of Standing Armies—The Feudal System—Mercenary Soldiers—Ancient Warfare—The Mutiny Act—The Secretary for War—The Staff—Cavalry—Infantry—Quartering of Troops—Camps—Purchase System—Price of Commissions—Pay of Officers—Brevet Rank—Recruiting—Pay of Privates—Dragoon Regiments—Names of Regiments—The Royal Artillery—The Royal Engineers—Precedence of Corps—Local Regiments—Courts Martial—Order of the Bath—Victoria Cross—Decorations—Pensions and Rewards—The Militia—The Yeomanry.

THE force maintained for the defence of this kingdom and its numerous dependencies against foreign attack, for the support of order at home, and for the security of our vast commerce, spreading over the entire surface of the globe, consists principally of THE ARMY and THE NAVY.

In treating of the first of these, I propose to commence by telling you something about the origin of a standing army in this country, and then to explain its composition and management.

I have already described how the military service of our ancestors was constituted under the feudal system. In the rude ages in which it existed, the force it provided was sufficient in every respect to protect our shores. All persons holding *knights fees* (of which there were more than 60,000 in England alone), were bound to be in readiness to attend their sovereign for forty days' service every year. Those who were unable or unwilling to take up arms were obliged to provide efficient substitutes, so that when a rebellion broke out, or an invasion was threatened, an army of 60,000 men could be brought into the field with very little delay, and no expense to the Crown. There were few fortified places in those days, and campaigns were not planned upon scientific principles. The contending forces usually attacked each other without delay, and the cause for which they fought was generally won and lost within the forty days. If the war was of longer duration, the feudal militia were entitled to return to their homes, or, continuing to serve, to be paid by the sovereign.

When our kings of the house of Plantagenet began their foreign wars, and encountered the partially trained soldiers of France, they found that they required more continuous and experienced services from their subjects than the Feudal system could provide. They therefore began to commute the military services of their *tenants in capite* for a money payment, or *scutage*, as it was termed, charged upon every knight's fee. Thus, when Henry II. was about to engage in hostilities against the Count of Toulouse, in 1159, instead of requiring all his vassals to accompany him, he imposed upon them a scutage, which produced a sum equal to 2,700,000*l*. of the money of the present day, with which he provided himself with an army accustomed to the march, and to be relied upon on the battle-field, and thus gained much popularity from those of his subjects who preferred remaining at home, in the pursuit of more peaceful avocations. At last money payments were entirely substituted for feudal services, which were finally abolished by the statute 12 Charles II. c. 24.

Philip Augustus of France was the first king who established an army of paid troops, in no way connected with the feudal militia, to protect his throne and humbler subjects from the lawlessness and tyranny of his great vassals. From the fact of their receiving money, they were called *Soldati* (whence our word "soldier,") derived from *soldo*, the Italian for *pay*. Several of our English sovereigns also maintained similar bodies of mercenaries, and paid them out of the revenues of the vast estates belonging to the Crown. Regular garrisons were kept in the Tower of London, the Castle of Dover, and in the Marches along the Scottish border,—posts of great military importance, where the presence of trained soldiers was always required; but with these exceptions the troops I have mentioned were only raised for some special purpose, and were disbanded as soon as the occasion for which they were embodied had passed.

Until the reign of Charles VII. of France, what we now designate a *standing army*—that is, a body of soldiers trained and paid by government, and kept under arms during peace for the defence of the State—was unknown. By this time the invention of gunpowder had entirely swept away the ancient plan of making war. As long as personal courage, strength and daring, decided the fate of a battle, war had great charms for noble knights who fought each one at his own expense, on horseback, cased in armour, and were always the principal combatants. Intellectual employment was almost unknown in those days, war and the chase being considered the only pursuits worthy the attention of a gentleman. But the introduction of firearms, especially artillery, deprived brute force and valour of their exclusive importance. It was one thing, encased in proof mail, to ride amongst an undisciplined and almost unarmed herd of leather-clad countrymen, and to mow them down with two-handed swords; but to charge a line of sturdy pikemen, supported by a rear rank of musketeers, whose bullets sent horse and rider rolling in the dust before the latter had the opportunity of striking a blow, was a very different state of affairs. Generals began to see the necessity for regular tactics under these new conditions. A crowd of armed men, each one fighting for himself, was no longer of any use in settling the disputes of nations. A military machine that could be directed with exact and steady action by the master-mind of the commander, was required. To produce this, practice, training and strict and unquestioning obedience were demanded, and the presence of a lower order of men was required in the ranks. The great importance of regular infantry became every day more and more apparent; war was reduced to a science, and standing armies were established throughout the continent of Europe.

The origin of our own present standing army dates as far back as 1660, when Charles II. formed two regiments of guards, one of horse and one of foot, and with these (and some other troops brought over from abroad) he organized a force of 5000 men. This number was increased during the reign of James II. to 30,000 soldiers. The embodiment of this army was, however, never sanctioned by Parliament; the king raised it by his own authority, and paid it out of the civil list by wrongfully appropriating money granted for other purposes. With this force he hoped to awe his subjects into submitting to the unconstitutional encroachments which had sent his father to the block. The hope, however, was a delusive one. So treacherous and fickle was his conduct, that civilians and the military made common cause against him, and no sooner had the Prince of Orange landed, than, as you know, the army joined his standard almost to a man.

But the danger which our forefathers thus escaped was a great one, and one which they were determined not to risk again. If you will turn back to my Letter in which I gave you some extracts from the Bill of Rights, you will see that a standing army cannot be maintained without the consent of Parliament. This is practically given by passing the *Mutiny Act*, in which the number of soldiers to be employed, the terms upon which they shall be enlisted, the offences for which they shall be punished, and the manner in which they shall be billeted, paid and pensioned, is laid down. The discipline of the army is regulated by the Articles of War, which are issued by the Crown in conformity with the Mutiny Act, and printed with it.

You will remember my telling you that the

sovereign is the head of the army; but military matters are managed entirely by the Secretary-of-State for War, and the Commander-in-chief of the Forces.

It is impossible to define with any great exactness the functions of the Secretary-of-State for War, as they seem to be mixed up with those of the Commander-in-chief in a not very comprehensible manner. This much, however, is clear, that the former arranges the number of men that Parliament is to be called upon to provide for, and forms the estimates accordingly; decides what troops are to be sent abroad in time of war; appoints the generals who are to command them; and is the constitutional medium between the Government and the army. The Commander-in-chief is responsible for the discipline and recruiting of the army. He is assisted by several subordinate officers, such as—

The Adjutant-General, who has the superintendence of all matters relating to what is called the *personnel* of the army; he is the channel through which all officers communicate with the Commander-in-chief: and all instructions, regulations and orders relative to the recruiting, organization and discipline of the army, and applications for leave of absence, come through him. He regulates also the employment of officers upon the staff, &c.

The Quartermaster-general, whose duty it is to prescribe, map out, and plan routes of marches; to pitch camps and find quarters for the troops; to manage their embarkation and disembarkation; to provide the means of transport for their stores, &c.

The Paymaster-general, who distributes the pay of the army.

The Commissary General supplies the troops with stores and provisions.

Each of these officers has a host of subordinates and clerks to transact the business of his department.

The British army consists of cavalry, infantry, artillery, and engineers. That portion of it called *the Guards*, or the "Household troops,"* as they

---

* The present strength of the Household troops is:—

Foot Guards, 3 regiments, having 7 battalions, 6300 men, inclusive of 257 officers.

Cavalry, 3 regiments, 1320 men, inclusive of 99 officers.

There are two other corps attached to the person of the sovereign, and which are rarely employed but at levees and other ceremonials; but these can scarcely be considered, like the Household troops, to form part of the army. The first is styled the corps of "Gentlemen-at-arms," and consists of a captain, lieutenant, standard-bearer, paymaster, clerk of the cheque or adjutant, a harbinger, and forty gentlemen. The other is called the "Yeomen of the guard," or, in common parlance, "Beefeaters," who until very lately have worn a singular costume, the

are also termed, because they guard the palaces and person of the sovereign, comprises the Grenadier, Coldstream, and Scots Fusileer regiments of Foot Guards; the 1st and 2nd regiments of Life Guards, and the Royal Horse Guards, or Blues. The three latter, which are cavalry, greatly distinguished themselves in the Peninsular war, as well as at Waterloo, but they have not been employed on foreign service since 1815. The strength of our regiments varies according to circumstances. At present an ordinary regiment of cavalry on home service consists of eight troops of fifty men each, officered as follows:—

1 Colonel. This is a mere titular rank, held by some distinguished general, who, beyond receiving the pay of the post, has very little to do with the regiment.

1 Lieutenant-colonel, who commands it.

1 Major.

8 Captains.

8 Lieutenants, } one of whom is adjutant.
8 Cornets,

1 Paymaster.

1 Quartermaster.

---

fashion of which had not been altered since the days of Henry VIII. This corps consists of 100 men, with the following officers: Captain, lieutenant, ensign, and two exons or corporals.

1 Ridingmaster.
1 Surgeon.
1 Assistant-surgeon.
1 Veterinary surgeon.

Nearly all the infantry regiments have at present two battalions. The regiment has but one colonel (in the infantry as in the cavalry a mere titular rank). Each battalion, which consists of twelve companies of 100 men each (when at full strength), is officered by—

1 Lieutenant-colonel.
2 Majors.
12 Captains.
15 Lieutenants, } one of whom is adjutant.
10 Ensigns,
1 Quartermaster.
1 Paymaster.
1 Instructor of musketry.
1 Surgeon.
2 Assistant-surgeons.

When a cavalry, or infantry, regiment is serving in India, it has two lieutenant-colonels; and the former also has one, and the latter two, additional assistant-surgeons. Regiments in India were paid by the East India Company, not by this nation, and received extra pay to place them upon an equality with its own army. Officers below the rank of captain are called *subalterns;* majors, lieutenant-colonels, and colonels, *field officers;* and all above the latter grade, *General officers.*

When a regiment of cavalry, or an infantry battalion, is sent abroad, two troops or companies remain behind, under a major, to form the *depôt*, which is to supply vacancies, &c. The remainder are called the *service* troops, or companies.

When peace was proclaimed after the great war with France, and the army returned, it was for awhile popular enough; but soon afterwards great political agitation took place—to such an extent, indeed, that for a time the *Habeas Corpus* Act was suspended, and our soldiers were scattered in small bodies over the country to act as police and check disturbances, particularly in Ireland. It was for a long time deemed impolitic to familiarize the English people with the display of soldiers massed together, and it was hoped that, by their dispersion in detachments, the existence of a standing army might be almost ignored. This concession to popular prejudices, which were not unreasonably founded, combined with other politic and conciliatory measures, eventually restored confidence, and soldiers ceased to be regarded as obnoxious agents of unconstitutional power. The troops, meanwhile, from being cooped up in small detachments, had lost much of their former efficiency; and it was found that, when occasionally brought together to execute manœuvres of any importance, they were strange to such duties, and unhandy in the performance of them. It was then felt that, if suddenly called upon to meet a foreign foe, an army collected of such raw materials would be no fair match for Continental troops trained to act together in large bodies—comprising every description of force, and forming complete armies. To remedy this defect, camps were subsequently formed, first at Chobham, and afterwards at Aldershot, Shorncliffe, and the Curragh in Ireland, and occasionally for siege operations at Chatham, where our soldiers were enabled to practise manœuvring in large bodies, and rehearse some of the ordinary operations of a campaign, and the attack and defence of fortified places. When two or more regiments act together, they form what is called a *brigade*, and are commanded usually by the senior Lt.-Col. as *brigadier*. Two or more brigades form a *division*, and several divisions an *army*.

Officers in the Guards, and cavalry and infantry of the Line, obtain their first and subsequent commissions up to the rank of major either by gift and promotion by the commander-in-chief, in the name of the sovereign, or by purchase from some of their comrades who have bought their commissions and wish to dispose of them. Thus, if the major wishes to sell, the senior captain who is ready and able to purchase the step does so; the senior lieutenant buys the vacant captain's commission; and so on down to the ensign or cornet, who sells the rank from which he is promoted to the aspirant for military fame who wishes to enter the service. But no officer can be advanced in this way without the approbation of the commander-in-chief, or until he has served a certain time in the rank from which he wishes to rise. Candidates for first commissions must pass an examination before they are allowed to enter the army.

There is no purchasing above the rank of major.

Much has been said about the injustice of this system of promotion, and as much urged in its support. To do away with it, the nation must be prepared to buy up all the commissions acquired under it, which are as much the private property of the officers who hold them as their swords. The leaning of the military authorities towards a gradual reform of the purchase system may, however, be inferred, from the great number of officers who now enter the army as ensigns without purchase. Our regimental system is agreed upon all hands to be more perfect than that of any foreign army, and although it may work injustice to individuals in some cases, it would be rash to make any sudden change, the introduction of which might impair the present efficiency and soldier-like spirit of our regimental officers.

It is essential, however, in reflecting upon this subject, to bear in mind that in the scientific branches of the army—the Engineers and Artillery, as well as the corps of Royal Marines—promotion is obtained by seniority, and that purchase in them is unknown. These corps cannot be surpassed for steady conduct and efficiency.

The following tables show the value of the commissions of regimental officers, and their pay per diem :—

PRICE OF COMMISSIONS.

Rank.	Life Guards.	Horse Guards.	Dragoon Guards and Dragoons.	Foot Guards.	Regiments of the Line.	Fusileer Regiments and Rifle Corps.
	£	£	£	£	£	£
Major............	5,350	5,350	4,575	8,330	3,200	3,200
Captain..........	3,500	3,500	3,225	4,800	1,800	1,800
Lieutenant......	1,785	1,600	1,190	2,050	700	700
2nd Lieutenant.	...	...	...	...	...	500
Cornet...........	1,260	1,200	840	...	...	...
Ensign...........	...	...	...	...	450	...

DAILY PAY OF OFFICERS.

Rank of Officer.	Life Guards and Horse Guards.	Foot Guards.	Dragoon Guards and Dragoons.	Foot.	Royal Artillery. Horse.	Royal Artillery. Foot.	Royal Engineers.
	£ s. d.	£ s. d.	£ s. d.	£ s. d.	£ s. d.	£ s. d.	£ s. d.
Colonel-commandant	...	...	...	...	3 0 0	2 14 9¼	2 14 9¼
Colonel	1 9 2	1 6 9	1 3 0	0 17 0	1 12 4	1 6 3	1 6 3
Lieutenant-colonel	1 4 5	1 3 0	0 19 3	0 16 1	1 7 1	0 13 1	0 18 1
Major	0 15 1	0 15 6	0 14 7	0 11 7			
Captain				0 13 7	0 16 1	0 11 1	0 11 1
Ditto with Brevet rank	0 10 4	0 7 4	0 9 0	0 6 6	0 18 1	0 13 1	0 13 1
Lieutenant				0 6 6	0 8 10	0 6 10	0 6 10
Ditto after 7 years' service	0 8 0	0 5 6	0 8 6	0 7 6	0 10 10	0 7 10	0 7 10
Cornet, Ensign, and 2nd Lieutenant			0 12 6	0 5 3		0 5 7	0 5 7
Paymaster, On appointment			0 15 6	0 12 6			
After 5 years' service, 15			0 17 6	0 15 6			
,, 20 ,,			1 0 6	0 17 6			
,, 25 ,,			1 2 6	1 2 6			
Adjutant			0 10 6	0 3 6*	0 10 8†	0 8 6†	
Quarter-master, On appointment	0 13 0	0 10 0	0 8 6	0 8 6			0 8 0
,, After 10 years' service, 15	0 9 6	0 6 6	0 10 6	0 8 6	0 10 10	0 7 10	
Surgeon-major		0 8 6	0 12 0	0 10 0			
Surgeon	0 13 0	0 10 0	0 13 0	0 13 0		0 13 0	
After 10 years' service	0 15 0	0 19 9	0 15 0	0 15 0		0 15 0	
,, 20 ,,	0 19 0	0 13 0	0 19 0	0 19 0		0 19 0	
,, 25 ,,	1 2 0	0 15 0	1 2 0	1 2 0		1 2 0	
Assistant Surgeon	0 8 0	0 19 0	0 8 0	0 7 6		0 7 6	
After 10 years' service	0 11 0	1 2 0	0 11 0	0 10 0		0 10 0	
Veterinary Surgeon	0 9 0	0 7 6	0 8 0	...	0 10 0		
After 3 years' service, 10	0 10 0	0 10 0	0 10 0	...	0 10 0		
,, 20 ,,	0 12 0	...	0 12 0	...	0 15 0		
,, 25 ,,	0 15 0	...	0 15 0	...			
	0 17 6	...	0 17 6	...			

* In addition to his pay as a subaltern.   † If 2nd Captain, 17s. 9d.   ‡ If 2nd Captain, 12s. 9d.

The officers of the Foot Guards enjoy a peculiar privilege, which entitles them to an accession of army rank; so that whilst in their own regiments they are respectively captains, lieutenants, &c., in the army at large they take a step higher, and rank accordingly as lieutenant-colonels, majors, captains, &c. What is called *Brevet rank* is given to officers in all branches of the army as a reward for brilliant and lengthened service; and when such nominal rank has been held for a certain number of years, it is usually converted into substantial rank.

When officers desire to retire from active service on account of ill health, wounds, &c., or when the strength of a regiment is reduced, they are, on obtaining permission from the authorities, put upon *half-pay*, which is a little more than a moiety of the full pay of their rank; they are, however, liable to be called upon to resume their duties.

The British army is the only force in Europe that is composed of volunteers. The great military forces of the Continent depend almost wholly upon conscription; but in our service the ranks are filled by voluntary enlistment, and recruiting parties are stationed in all our large towns expressly for that purpose. The recruit receives a sum of money as *bounty*, and is provided with a *kit* of clothing and necessaries. When enlisted he is taken before a justice of the peace, who is directed by the Mutiny

Act to put to him certain questions, to give him time to reflect upon what he has done, and to prevent hasty or incautious enlistment. If he should change his mind, he is dismissed upon paying a fine of twenty shillings, popularly called *smart money;* but if he does not, he is *attested*, and after that, should he abscond, he is considered and punished as a deserter. If his conduct be good, he may rise to be a non-commissioned, and even a commissioned officer. In the latter case, he is presented in the cavalry with 150*l.*, and in the infantry with 100*l.*, to purchase an outfit.

The following is a table of the pay of non-commissioned officers and privates, from which is deducted a certain sum for their clothing and food :—

Rank.	Household Cavalry.	Foot Guards.	Line.	Royal Artillery.		Engineers.	Dragoon Guards and Dragoons.
				Horse.	Foot.		
	s. d.	s. d.	s. d.	s. d.	s. d.	s. d.	s. d.
Sergeants..	2 8¼	2 2	2 0	3 0	2 10	3 0	3 0
Corporals..	...	1 5	1 4	2 4	2 2	2 4	1 7¼
Privates...	1 11¼	1 1	1 0	1 5½	1 3¼	1 5	1 3

Over and above all deductions, the private soldier of the Line has about threepence left to him to spend as he pleases. This may seem a small sum; but it must be remembered that his food and clothing are paid for, that he is provided with light, fire, and house-rent free, as well as medical attendance; and that, if he behaves himself well, he has good prospects of promotion, and the certainty of a pension for his latter days. The majority of men in the ranks of life from which he springs are certainly not so well off in many respects.

I will now return to the organization of the army. The cavalry are termed either *heavy* or *light*, according to the nature of their respective duties on service, and the manner in which they are mounted and armed. Our heavy cavalry, besides the three regiments of Household troops previously mentioned, consists of ten regiments, seven of which are known as "Dragoon Guards," and the other three as "Dragoons."* We have at present fifteen regiments of light cavalry, all officially styled "Light Dragoons." Of these, five regiments are *Lancers*, so called from the weapon with which they are armed—namely, the 5th, 9th, 12th, 16th, and 17th— and six *Hussars*, which name is derived from the Hungarian words *husz* (twenty), and *ar* (pay), because every twenty houses had to provide one horse soldier. The Hussar regiments are the 7th, 8th, 10th, 11th, 15th and 18th; the remaining four regiments have no other name than Light Dragoons.

* The term "dragoon" is derived from the Roman *draconarii*, who bore lances ornamented with the figure of a dragon, and were trained to fight both on horseback and on foot.

The *Military Train* is also a cavalry corps, its duties being to transport stores and munitions of war, to guard the baggage, &c. At present it numbers 107 officers and 1734 men.

Each regiment is known by its number, and many have a distinguishing name besides. Thus, in the cavalry the 1st Dragoon Guards are called "the King's;" the 4th Dragn. Guards, "the Royal Irish;" the 6th Dragn. Guards, "the Carbineers," from the weapon they carry; the 1st Dragoons are called "Royals;" the 2nd Drags. are the renowned "Scots Greys;" their old companions in glory, the 6th Drags. the "Inniskillens;" the 11th Light Drags. are "Prince Albert's Own Hussars." In the infantry, which consists of 100 regiments, the 1st Foot, formerly known as "the Royal Scots," is now styled "Royals;" the 3rd Foot, "the Buffs;" 4th Foot, "the King's Own;" 18th Foot, "the Royal Irish;" 23rd Foot, "the Welsh Fusileers;" 26th Foot, "the Cameronians;" 27th Foot, "Inniskillens;" 33rd Foot, "the Duke of Wellington's Own Regiment;" the 88th, "the Connaught Rangers;" the 100th Foot, just raised in Canada, "the Royal Canadian Regiment." There are seven Highland regiments*—viz., the 42nd, 72nd, 74th, 78th, 79th,

---

* Of these, five regiments wear the kilt—viz., the 42nd, 78th, 79th, 92nd, and 93rd; the other two wear the *trews*, or tartan trousors.

92nd, and 93rd; five Fusileers, the 5th, 7th, 21st, 23rd, and 87th; and nine Light Infantry regiments —viz., the 13th, 32nd, 43rd, 51st, 52nd, 68th, 71st (Highland), 85th, and 90th. The 60th Regiment, containing four battalions, is a Rifle corps; and there is also a distinct corps (not numbered) called the "Rifle Brigade," likewise consisting of four battalions. The first twenty-four regiments of foot now have two battalions each. When any augmentation of the army is required on the breaking out of war, &c., it is customary to raise a second battalion to existing regiments rather than to create new ones.

Every battalion of foot has two flags, the Queen's colour, or Union Jack, and the regimental colour, upon which is emblasoned the arms or crest of the corps, as well as the names of the victories to which it has contributed, inscribed under royal sanction. The standards of the cavalry bear similar honourable decorations.

The Artillery has become in recent warfare the most important arm of the military service. The Royal Artillery is divided into brigades, which are again subdivided into batteries. It numbers about 800 officers, 1500 non-commissioned officers, trumpeters, and drummers, and 20,000 rank and file. In the brigade of Horse Artillery there are 77 officers, 120 non-commissioned officers, &c., and 1700 privates. The gunners of the Royal Artillery ride upon the tumbrils of the pieces; those of the Horse Artillery are mounted, and follow them.

The Royal Engineers, the rank and file of which corps was formerly called the "Sappers and Miners," is also a most distinguished and useful branch of the service. It is charged with the construction of fortifications and entrenchments for the army in the field, and to carry on mining operations. It also conducts siege operations, constructs bridges and pontoons for crossing rivers, and other necessary works. At the commencement of the present year the Royal Engineers consisted of 401 officers, 374 non-commissioned officers, &c., and 3918 privates. Commissions in the Artillery and Engineers—constituting the scientific corps of the army—are now thrown open for public competition; but candidates must be nominated by the commander-in-chief before they can present themselves for examination. This proviso, however, seems only made to ensure the previous character of the applicant being creditable. These two branches of the service were formerly under the authority of the Board of Ordnance, but are now merged into the general management of the army.

PRECEDENCE OF CORPS.

The foregoing is an outline of the composition of the hard-worked army of Great Britain, which in turn is sent all over the world to protect her rights and interests.

The etiquette of the army as to regimental precedence observed when forming the line at reviews is as follows:—

1. The Artillery usually occupies both right and left flanks.

2. The Cavalry is posted next to the Artillery on the right.

3. The Foot Guards next to the Cavalry on the right.

4. The Infantry of the Line on the left of the Guards, according to the respective numbers of their regiments. When the Royal Marines form part of the line, their place is next after the 50th Regiment.

The number of men voted for the British army in the year 1865 was 142,477, at a total cost of 14,348,000*l*. This is, however, exclusive of between 70,000 and 80,000 men who are serving in India, and are maintained out of the revenues of that country.

In addition to the regular army we maintain some local corps, which serve in the colonies and foreign stations. These consist of—

Three regiments of blacks, which are recruited and stationed in the West India islands and on the coast of Africa.

Royal Malta Fencibles.
The Gold Coast Corps.
The St. Helena Regiment.
The Cape Mounted Rifles.
The Ceylon Rifles.
Royal Newfoundland Veteran Companies.
The Royal Canadian Rifle Regiment.

Offenders against military discipline are tried before *courts martial* composed of officers selected from the regiment or the garrison in which the prisoner serves. The Judge-Advocate General, who is a civilian nominated by Government, has the control of these tribunals. A Deputy Judge-Advocate, generally an officer, attends at every trial, and sees that it is conducted according to law. A member is appointed to preside, and the charge against the accused, which must be in proper form, is read over to him, and the evidence against and for him heard and reduced to writing. This done, the prisoner is ordered to withdraw, and the court deliberates upon its verdict, which, as well as the punishment to follow it, should it be one of "guilty," is decided by a majority. The "proceedings," comprising the charge and evidence, are then submitted to the general commanding the district, who either "approves and confirms them," or sends them back for further consideration, or sets them aside altogether. The result of the trial is not allowed to transpire, even to the prisoner, until this officer's decision is made known.

The rewards for long and meritorious service which are bestowed upon our brave defenders, form a more pleasing subject than the last: these are given in the shape of titles, pensions, promotions and decorations. The sovereign has, as you know, the right of bestowing any distinction upon a subject. Peerages and baronetcies are frequently given to the heroes of great military achievements, and the people of England are by no means backward in granting the substantial means necessary for keeping up those dignities, as witness the provision made for Marlborough and Wellington by a grateful nation, and in our time for Williams, the gallant defender of Kars, and for the son of the brave and lamented Havelock.

The *Order of the Bath* is a decoration much coveted by military and naval officers. There is also a civil branch of this Order for non-combatants; it is divided into three ranks :—

Knights Grand Crosses—G.C.B. ;

Knights Commanders—K.C.B. ; and
Companions—C.B.

The decoration is a star. The order of *St. Michael and St. George* is bestowed upon officers in the army and navy who have distinguished themselves in the Mediterranean.

But perhaps the most highly-prized decoration worn by our army and navy is the lately instituted *Victoria Cross.* This is a plain piece of bronze, but upon it is imprinted the magic motto, "*For Valour,*" and it is only awarded for the most devoted and daring bravery in the field.

Medals are often struck to commemorate successful actions or campaigns, and are distributed to, and worn by, all ranks that have taken part in them. The medal itself commemorates the campaign; and clasps are frequently added to the ribbon which suspends it, upon each of which is engraved the name of the particular action for which the wearer has received it.

Pensions are given to non-commissioned officers and privates, who from wounds or infirmity are no longer fit for service. *Out*-pensioners receive their pay, and live where they please. Some, the youngest and most vigorous of these, are enrolled for further service, if required, and are called out for exercise every year.

THE MILITIA.

In-pensioners are lodged and maintained in the Hospitals at Chelsea near London, and Kilmainham in Dublin.

I must now draw this very long Letter to a conclusion, although, perhaps, I have not told you all you might like to hear about our soldiers. But, before I close it, there is a force which I must not omit to describe, as it is the ancient constitutional guardian of our shores, and of late years has proved an admirable nursery for the regular army, I mean the *Militia*. This term, in its general sense, signifies the whole body of persons, stipendiary or not, who bear arms for the defence of the State; but now its meaning is restricted to the forces raised in our counties and commanded by their lords-lieutenant. Formerly the Militia was raised by ballot—every person upon whom the lot fell was bound to serve or find a substitute—but now its recruits are enlisted and bounty given to them as in the regular army. Every county has its regiment of Militia, the large ones having several: thus Middlesex has five, and Lancashire and Yorkshire eight apiece. Counties upon the sea-coast form regiments of artillery and rifles; those in the interior, infantry. These are generally called together once every year for training during a period of from twenty to twenty-seven days, or longer, at the option of the Government. Under recent Acts of Parliament the Militia may be permanently embodied, and even sent abroad. During the late war with Russia, many garrisons, both at home and in the Mediterranean, were manned by Militia regiments so embodied, much to their own credit and greatly to the advantage of the State, for we were thus enabled to withdraw the regular troops from those places, and to send them to reinforce our hard-worked battalions before Sebastopol. Moreover, the Militia supplied thousands of recruits for the line,—men who had had some experience of a soldier's life, liked it, and were already more than half-trained to their duties. The officers and men of the Militia, except the adjutant and staff, are only paid when called out for training, or as long as they are embodied. The commissions of the former are signed by the lord-lieutenant of the county, but the adjutant is appointed by the Queen. In England and Wales we have ninety-six regiments of Militia; in Scotland, seventeen; and in Ireland, forty-four. The army estimates provide 786,400*l.* for the disembodied militia in the year 1865-6. The number of men to be called up for 27 days' training is stated at 128,969.

A somewhat similarly constituted force to the Militia is the *Yeomanry*, but greatly subordinate to it in importance; one object for which it is kept up being apparently to provide certain country gentlemen with a showy uniform, wherewith to make a figure at court, instead of the unbecoming footman-like costume in which etiquette demands that simple gentlemen must appear at her Majesty's levees and drawing-rooms.

The last branch of the military service to which it is necessary for me to refer is the Volunteer force. Owing its origin to the dread of a French invasion, it has survived the cause from which it sprang, and has now become a permanent element in our system of national defence. At present it consists of about 160,000 men, who give their services gratuitously, although a small sum is annually voted by Parliament in order to defray a portion at least of the necessary expenses of the various corps.

LETTER XII.

THE NAVY.

Popularity of the Navy—Early History—Naval Ascendency—Prizes of War—Size of Men-of-War—The Board of Admiralty—Rating of Ships—Officers of a Man-of-War—Stations of Ships—Pay of Officers—Relative Army and Navy Rank—Commissions in the Navy—Pay of Warrant Officers—of Sailors—Pensioners—The Coast Guard—Royal Marines—Pay in the Marines.

THE navy of Great Britain is perhaps the most popular of our national forces, and deservedly so. Our army has won us honour and triumphs abroad, but it is to the navy that we owe our security at home. From the time when Lord Howard of Effingham, with his great sea captains Drake, Hawkins, and Frobisher, scattered before them the wrecks of the so-called "Invincible" Spanish Armada down to that eventful day when Nelson's victorious cannons roared in the Bay of Trafalgar, it has been our best bulwark against the invader, and but for our stout wooden walls, his devastating footsteps might even now be traced upon our pleasant pastures. The navy has never been looked upon with suspicion as a force which might be employed by an unconstitutional sovereign to curtail the liberties and rights of the people. On the contrary, save during that humiliating epoch in our history when our king was the pensioner of a French monarch, and applied to his vices and pleasures the sums which should have gone to maintain the fleet, it has been the special care both of governors and governed to keep up its strength and efficiency. In the year 1707 the House of Lords, in an address to Queen Anne, said "that the honour, security and wealth of this kingdom depend upon the protection and encouragement of trade and the improving and right encouraging its naval strength . . . *therefore we do, in the most earnest manner, beseech your majesty that the sea affairs may always be your first and most peculiar care.*" It will be an evil day for England when the principle laid down in this address is departed from.

Previous to the reign of Elizabeth our sovereigns had but few ships of war. The naval force collected to oppose the Armada was the largest armament that had ever been brought together under an English commander. It consisted of 176 ships and about 15,000 men. But of this fleet only 40 ships and 6000 sailors belonged to the royal navy; the rest were contributed by London, Bristol,

Yarmouth, the Cinque Ports, &c. The navy had not yet become a separate service and distinct profession. Our captains were soldiers or sailors as occasion required. At the battle of Flodden Field the admiral of England led the right wing of the army, and Lord Howard of Effingham was never bred up to the sea. The career of John Sheffield, Earl of Mulgrave, shows how naval appointments were made in the latter part of the sixteenth century. At the age of seventeen he volunteered to serve at sea against the Dutch, and after six weeks returned home to take the command of a troop of horse. Six years afterwards he was made captain of an eighty-four gun ship, although in the whole course of his life he had never been three months afloat. A short time afterwards he was given a regiment of foot! Under the first sovereigns of the house of Stuart our navy degenerated: but the vigorous and able administration of Oliver Cromwell speedily raised it to a magnitude and power hitherto unknown. He divided it into *rates* and *classes*, and under the command of Admiral Blake it not only equalled, but surpassed, the famous marine of Holland. James II.—himself a naval commander and his own Lord High Admiral—also paid great attention to marine affairs. At his abdication, the fleet amounted to 173 sail, measuring 101,892 tons, and having on board 6,930 guns and 42,000 seamen. Since this time the efficiency of the royal navy has steadily increased, and although there have been periods in which the combined fleets of France and Spain and other coalitions have deprived us for a short time of our ascendency, the victories of Rodney, Howe, Duncan, St. Vincent, and Nelson soon restored to us that sovereignty of the sea to which, from our extended empire, our enormous commerce,* and our maritime habits and prowess, we may still justly lay claim.

The following tables will show the triumphs of our gallant tars in the last wars, in which they took a principal part :—

Ships taken or destroyed by the Naval and Marine Forces of Great Britain in the French Revolutionary War ending 1802.

Force.	French.	Dutch.	Spanish.	Other Nations.	Total.
Ships of the Line	45	25	11	2	83
Fifty-gun ships	2	1	0	0	3
Frigates	133	31	20	7	191
Sloops, &c.	161	32	55	13	264
Grand Total	341	89	86	25	541

* Some idea may be formed of the gigantic extent of the British commercial marine, from the fact that in 1863 it comprised 20,877 vessels, of 4,795,279 tons, and manned by 184,727 sailors.

Number of Ships taken or destroyed in the War against Buonaparte ending 1814.

Force.	French.	Spanish.	Danish.	Russian.	American.	Total.
Ships of the Line	70	27	23	4	0	124
Fifty-gun ships	7	0	1	0	1	9
Frigates	77	36	24	6	5	148
Sloops, &c.	188	64	16	7	13	288
Grand Total...	342	127	64	17	19	569

It thus appears that in a period of about twenty-one years our fleet had taken or destroyed one thousand one hundred and ten ships of the navies of our enemies!

The introduction of steamers as ships of war has caused a great revolution in naval tactics. Formerly the main object of a commander was to get what is called the *weather gauge* of his enemy; that is to say, to sail on the side of him from which the wind is coming, so as to enable him to manœuvre round and *rake* him by sweeping the whole length of his decks with his guns in crossing his bow or stern. Steamers, however, are almost wholly independent of wind or tide, and screw-steamers combine the advantages of steaming with sailing. Our ships are now built very much larger, and carry more and much heavier guns than they did even twenty years ago; in fact, the largest ships-of-the-line with which Nelson and Collingwood fought would be considered as mere frigates in comparison with the mighty men-of-war of the present day. Nor is it merely in their size that the men-of-war of to-day differ from those of other times. Formerly, as I daresay you know, they were constructed of wood; but, in order to cope with the terribly destructive power of modern artillery, they are now covered with thick plates of iron, and, indeed, in most cases the ships of what may be called our effective fighting navy are entirely built of that material.

The general direction and control of all affairs connected with the royal navy is now entrusted by her Majesty to the Commissioners for discharging the duties of Lord High Admiral. From the reign of Queen Anne down to the present time, with the exception of a short period during which William IV., when Duke of Clarence, held it, that high office has never been entrusted to a single individual. The commission for performing its duties consists of the First Lord of the Admiralty—a cabinet minister—and from four to six junior lords. Civilians may be appointed to these posts, but at least two of the lords are always naval officers.

Practically speaking, all the power and authority of the *Board of Admiralty*, as the commission is sometimes called, is vested in the First Lord. Its powers are extensive and important. By its orders all ships are built, repaired, fitted for sea, put in commission and out of commission, armed, stored, and provisioned, despatched on home or foreign service, broken up, and sold. All appointments and removals of commissioned and warrant officers are made by its orders. All promotions in the several ranks (except to that of Admiral, to which Captains are promoted by seniority), all honours, pensions, and gratuities, are granted upon its recommendation. All returns from the fleet, and everything that relates to the order and discipline of every ship, are sent in and reported to this board. The annual estimates of the expenses of the navy are prepared by the Lords Commissioners, and are laid before Parliament by the First Lord, or by the Secretary to the Admiralty. The sums voted are expended by or under the direction of the board. They also have the direction of all buildings and machinery in the dockyards, and no new inventions can be adopted and no alterations made in them without their sanction.

The ships of the royal navy were, by an order in council dated 1816, divided into six rates,* or classes according to their size, &c., as follows:—

First-rates.—All three-decked ships.

Second-rates.—One of her Majesty's yachts, and two-decked ships carrying not less than 80 guns, or which have a complement of not less than 750 men.

Third-rates.—Her Majesty's other yachts, and all such vessels as may bear the flag or pendant of any admiral, or captain superintendent of a royal dockyard, and all ships carrying under 80, and not less than 70, guns, or which have a complement under 750, and not less than 620, men.

Fourth-rates.—Ships carrying under 70, and not less than 50, guns, or the complements of which are under 620, and not less than 450, men.

Fifth-rates.—All ships under 50 guns, and not less than 30, or the complements of which are under 450, and not less than 300, men. And

Sixth-rates—which comprise three classes:

1. All other ships bearing a captain.

2. Sloops—comprising bomb ships, and all other vessels with commanders.

3. All other ships commanded by lieutenants, and having complements of not less than 60 men.

---

* This classification is still nominally in force; but it is practically obsolete, since it does not deal with the most important vessels of our existing navy—the iron-clads.

OFFICERS OF A MAN OF WAR.

A First-rate has usually on board the following officers:—

1 Captain.
1 Commander.
6 Lieutenants, or more.
1 Master.
1 Captain of Marines.
2 Lieutenants of Marines.
1 Chaplain.
1 Surgeon.
2 Mates.
1 Assistant Surgeon.
1 Paymaster.
1 Second Master.
1 Chief Engineer (if a Steamer).
1 Naval Instructor.
Midshipmen and naval cadets according to circumstances.

If the ship carries the flag of an admiral, there are besides that officer his flag-lieutenant and secretary, on board.

Ships of lesser rates are officered in like manner; the number of lieutenants, &c., being proportioned to their complement, and number of guns.

The following is an extract from a return of the number of our iron-plated ships and batteries in June, 1865:—

NAMES.	No. of Guns.	Tonnage.	Horse Power.
Afloat.			
Black Prince	41	6,109	1,250
Warrior	40	6,109	1,250
Defence	18	3,720	600
Resistance	18	3,710	600
Achilles	26	6,121	1,250
Hector	20	4,089	800
Valiant	24	4,076	800
Minotaur	26	6,621	1,350
Agincourt	26	6,621	1,350
Royal Oak	35	4,056	800
Prince Consort	31	4,045	1,000
Caledonia	30	4,125	1,000
Ocean	23	4,047	1,000
Royal Alfred	18	4,068	800
Zealous	20	3,716	800
Bellerophon	16	4,270	1,000
Lord Clyde	24	4,067	1,000
Lord Warden	24	4,080	1,000
Pallas	6	2,126	600
Favorite	10	2,094	400
Research	4	1,253	200
Enterprise	4	993	160
Royal Sovereign	5	3,765	800
Prince Albert	4	2,511	500
Scorpion	4	1,857	350
Wyvern	4	1,857	350
Building.			
Northumberland	26	6,621	1,350
Viper	4	737	160
Vixen	4	754	160
Waterwitch	4	777	167
Penelope	10	2,947	600
Hercules	Design not completed.		

NAMES.	No. of Guns.	Tonnage.	Horse Power.
Floating Batteries.			
Erebus	16	1,954	200
Terror	16	1,971	200
Thunderbolt	16	1,973	200
Etna	16	1,588	200
Thunder	14	1,469	150

According to the Navy Estimates for the year 1865-6, the force to be maintained will be 69,750 officers, seamen, and boys, including 17,000 Marines. The total cost of the navy, inclusive of building stores, and various other items for the year, is stated in the estimates at 10,392,224*l*.

There are three gradations of admirals in the royal navy, viz.: *Admirals, Vice-Admirals,* and *Rear-Admirals.* Admirals bear their flags at the main-top-gallant mast head; vice-admirals at the fore-top-gallant mast head; and rear-admirals at the mizen-top-gallant mast head.

All admirals are called *flag-officers.*

I gave you a tabular statement of the pay of officers in the army; I am afraid I cannot put the full pay of the officers of the navy into the same shape, as there are, as you will see, so many variations in its amounts. They are as follow:—

MILITARY BRANCH.

	£	s.	d.	
ADMIRAL OF THE FLEET ...	2,190	0	0	per annum.
ADMIRAL	1,825	0	0	,,
VICE-ADMIRAL...	1,460	0	0	,,
REAR-ADMIRAL, and COMMODORE of the 1st Class	1,095	0	0	,,
CAPTAIN OF THE FLEET ...	1,095	0	0	,,
COMMODORE of the 2nd Class, If commanding in chief, (in addition to his pay as Captain)	365	0	0	,,
If not commanding in chief (in addition to his pay as Captain)	182	10	0	,,
CAPTAINS,				
To the first 70	600	14	7	,,
To the next 100	500	7	1	,,
To the remainder	399	19	7	,,
COMMANDER,				
In all rates	365	0	0	,,
LIEUTENANT,				
In command of a ship ...	200	15	0	,,
All others	182	10	0	,,

PAY OF OFFICERS.

MASTER,

	£	s.	d.	
After 25 years' service	365	0	0	per annum.
„ 20 „ „	328	10	0	„
„ 15 „ „	273	15	3	„
„ 10 „ „	219	0	0	„
„ 6 „ „	200	15	0	„
All others	182	10	0	„

SECOND MASTER,

If qualified for a Master	136	17	6	„
If not qualified for ditto	91	5	0	„

MIDSHIPMAN	31	18	9	„
MASTER'S ASSISTANT	47	2	11	„
NAVAL CADET	16	14	7	„

CIVIL BRANCH.

PAYMASTER, 1st Class	600	7	1	„
„ 2nd Class	474	10	0	„
„ 3rd Class	349	15	10	„
„ 4th Class	249	8	4	„

CHIEF ENGINEER,

After 25 years' service, if qualified for 1st or 2nd rates	365	0	0	„
After 20 years' service, ditto	328	10	0	„
„ 15 „ „	282	17	6	„
„ 10 „ „	237	5	0	„
„ 5 „ „	209	17	6	„
Under 5 „ „	191	12	6	„

PAY OF OFFICERS. 135

	£	s.	d.	
ASSISTANT ENGINEER, 1st Class	136	17	6	per annum.
,, ,, 2nd Class	109	10	0	,,

CHAPLAIN,
    According to length of service, from ... 182 10 0 to 200 15 0 ,,

SURGEON,
    According to length of service, from ... 273 15 0 to 456 5 0 ,,

ASSISTANT SURGEON,
    According to length of service, from ... 182 10 0 to 237 5 0 ,,

NAVAL INSTRUCTOR,
    After 20 years' service £237 5 0 per ann. ⎫
    ,, 15 ,, 209 17 6 ,, ⎬ With a tuition allowance for each young gentleman instructed of 5l.
    ,, 10 ,, 182 10 0 ,,
    ,, 7 ,, 155 2 6 ,,
    ,, 3 ,, 136 17 6 ,,
    Under 3 ,, 127 15 0 ,, ⎭

CLERK 73 0 0

I have not included in the foregoing statement all the officers and clerks of the civil branch, but just enough of them to give you a sufficient notion of the rate of pay of officers in the navy.

The following table will show you the relative rank of officers in the army and navy :—

1. The Admiral of the Fleet ranks with a Field Marshal in the army.

2. Admirals	rank with	Generals.
3. Vice-Admirals	,,	Lieut.-Generals.
4. Rear-Admirals	,,	Major-Generals.
5. Commodores of the First Class, Second Class, and the Director General of the Medical Department of the Navy.	,,	Brigadier-Generals.
6. Captains after 3 years' service	,,	Colonels.
7. Other Captains	,,	Lieut.-Colonels.
8. Commanders, Secretaries to Flag Officers, and Deputy Inspectors General of Hospitals and Fleets … … …	,,	Majors.
9. Lieutenants, Masters of the Fleet, Inspectors of machinery afloat, Masters, Chief Engineers, Chaplains, Secretaries, Surgeons, Paymasters,	,,	Captains.
10. Mates, Assistant Surgeons,	,,	Lieutenants.
11. Second Masters, Passed Clerks, Midshipmen,	,,	Ensigns.

But no officer of the navy can assume command of land forces, neither can an officer of the army assume command of any ship.

The number of officers employed and unemployed, on the active list of the Royal Navy on the 1st of July, 1865, is given as follows:—

Flag Officers	81
Captains	300
Commanders	399
Lieutenants	733
Masters	244
Engineers	229
Second Masters	141
Chaplains	156
Naval Instructors	102
Surgeons	287
Assistant Surgeons	285
Paymasters	299
Assistant Paymasters	277

In addition to these there are a large number of officers (no longer available for active service), on the reserved and retired lists.

Commissions and promotions in the navy are not obtained by purchase, but young gentlemen enter this service as naval cadets, after passing an examination; and promotion to every subsequent step up to the rank of captain, must be preceded by a similar test of efficiency.

Sailors for manning the navy were not long ago obtained, during time of war, by *impressment*. Armed parties, under the command of an officer, called *press-gangs*, used to land at a port and carry off by force any seafaring men that they could lay their hands on, to serve in the royal navy. Under laws, now repealed, justices of the peace had power to give rogues and vagabonds the alternative of going to jail, or serving in the fleet! But no such measures are now resorted to; seamen, like soldiers, enter the Queen's service at their own free will, and receive *bounty* for so doing.

The pay of some of the warrant, and petty officers, answering to the non-commissioned officers of the army, and of sailors in the royal navy, is as follows:—

Warrant Officers.

Gunner, Boatswain, and Carpenter,		£	s.	d.	
	1st Class	164	5	0	per annum.
	2nd „	127	15	0	„
	3rd „	109	10	0	„

Petty Officers.

	£	s.	d.	
Chief Gunner's Mate, Chief Boatswain's Mate, Chief Carpenter's Mate, Ship's Cook,	44	2	1	„
Gunner's Mate, Captain of the Fore-top, Captain of the Hold,	39	10	0	„
Coxswain of the Barge, Captain of the Mast, Yeoman of the Signals,	34	19	7	„

PENSIONERS.

	£	s.	d.	
Stoker and Coal Trimmer	36	10	0	per annum.
Able Seaman	28	17	11	,,
Ordinary Seaman	22	16	3	,,
Boy, 1st Class	10	12	11	,,
Boy, 2nd Class	9	2	6	,,

Pensions are granted to all seamen discharged after twenty-one years' service for *any cause* other than misconduct. Sailors who engage for what is called *continuous service*, receive the pay I have set against their names as long as they remain in the service. Those who enlist otherwise receive full pay whilst their ships are *in commission*, when the ship is put *out of commission* they are paid off and discharged. It is in the discretion of the Board of Admiralty to award pensions under any circumstances.

Pensioners are divided into two classes, *in* and *out* pensioners of Greenwich Hospital. This magnificent building, once a royal palace, was appropriated in the reign of William III. as an asylum for seamen, who by wounds, age, or accident, have become unfit for further active service. When, after the famous battle of La Hogue, crowds of maimed and suffering sailors were cast upon their country, Queen Mary, the good and gentle wife of that monarch, showed great solicitude for their welfare, and wished to found an institution to relieve and maintain them. Upon her death, which took place soon afterwards, her sorrowing husband set apart the palace of Greenwich for that purpose. It has been greatly improved and enlarged since then, and it stands a national memorial of one of our greatest naval victories, and a monument to the memory of her who, amidst the exultations that followed the triumph, did not forget those whose blood had been shed to gain it.

The rules and provisions for the enforcement of discipline and good order in the navy are embodied in an Act of Parliament passed in the 19th year of George III., and offenders against them are tried by courts-martial, nearly in the same way as in the army, except that the court must be held in a ship *afloat*, and that its decision does not require confirmation, and is made public directly it is delivered.

The *Coast Guard* until lately was partly under the control of the Admiralty, and partly under that of the Excise. It was manned in a great measure, and commanded, by men and officers from the navy, but was a separate service. It is now incorporated with the royal navy. Its duties are to capture smugglers and to prevent the landing of contraband goods. To carry out these, small fast-sailing vessels, ranging from one hundred and fifty down to twenty-three tons, carrying from five to thirty-two men, and commanded by lieutenants in the navy, or by civilians from the merchant service, cruise about our coasts. Stations also are formed on shore from which patrols are sent out, and where watch is kept day and night.

The *Coast Volunteers* are a sort of seafaring militia, trained for service with the navy in case of emergency.

The *Royal Naval Reserve* consists of volunteers from the mercantile service who undergo a certain amount of training annually in time of peace, and hold themselves at the disposal of the country in time of war. Merchant vessels, whose crews comprise a certain proportion of naval reserve men, have a right to carry the Blue ensign, ordinary merchantmen being restricted to the use of the Red ensign; while men-of-war bear the White ensign.

The corps of *Royal Marines* is under the control of the Board of Admiralty, and forms part of the establishment of the navy. It serves on board our ships, and garrisons the royal dockyards. The date of the formation of this force has not been exactly ascertained: we first hear of it in the year 1684.

It is now separated into two sections, the Marine Light Infantry and the Royal Marine Artillery: the former consists of four divisions, which are stationed respectively, at Chatham, Portsmouth, Plymouth, and Woolwich, and number more than 100 companies. There are thirteen companies of Marine Artillery, the head-quarters of which are at Portsmouth. The following is a table of the annual pay of officers and men in the Marines:—

OFFICERS.	Light Infantry. £ s. d.	Artillery. £ s. d.
1st Colonel Commandant	702 12 6	—
2nd Colonel Commandant	365 0 0	476 1 3
Lieutenant Colonel	310 5 0	326 19 7
Captain, having higher rank by brevet	247 17 11	257 0 5
Captain	211 7 11	220 10 5
1st Lieutenant, after 7 years' service.	136 17 6	142 19 2
,, under ,,	118 12 6	124 14 0
Adjutant, besides pay as Lieutenant.	118 12 6	—
2nd Lieutenant	95 16 3	101 16 11
Cadet	66 18 4	—

NON-COMMISSIONED OFFICERS AND PRIVATES.

Sergeant Major	54 15 0	74 18 0¼
Sergeant	33 9 2	44 9 8¼
Corporal, 1st Class	27 7 6	42 11 8
,, 2nd ,,	24 6 8	39 10 10
Private, 1st Class	21 5 10	26 4 8½
,, 2nd ,,	18 5 0	23 3 0

Gentlemen enter this service as cadets, and are instructed in their profession on board *The Excellent*, gunnery ship, at Portsmouth. The most proficient are chosen for the Marine Artillery, the junior officers of which force are selected from the most capable of their rank in the general body of the Royal Marines.

Promotion in this corps goes entirely by seniority.

All the rewards for long and distinguished services and bravery, that I mentioned in my letter upon the army, are open to officers in the navy and Marines.

LETTER XIII.

THE LAW.

The Common Law—Statute Law—Civil Law—Roman Civil Law—Equity—Conflicts of Law and Equity—New Procedure—Interpretation of the Law—The Sheriff, his Office and Responsibility in executing and enforcing the Law.

I SHALL now proceed to the second division of my subject, the

"PRACTICE OF THE LAW OF ENGLAND."

Our law is of two kinds, the *unwritten*, or Common Law, made up of ancient customs,* either *general*, affecting the whole kingdom, or *special*, having force only in particular places; and the *written*, or Statute Law, made and altered from time to time in Parliament, as I have described in a former Letter. The Common, and the Statute Law, are declared and interpreted by the decisions of the judges contained in the law reports.

The law thus composed may again be divided under two heads: the *Civil Law*, which relates to the rights of the people amongst themselves, giving remedies by *action*, in which the person aggrieved is called the *plaintiff*, and he against whom the

---

* A "custom," to be good in point of law, must have existed from time immemorial.

proceedings are taken the *defendant;* and the Criminal Law, which is put in operation by *prosecution*, in the name of the Sovereign, against evil-doers.

A particular code of Civil Law derived from the Roman Civil Law, and some portions of the Roman Canon Law, is adopted in the Ecclesiastical and Admiralty Courts, and the Courts of Probate and Matrimonial Causes, which severally decide cases relating to the discipline of the clergy, and the regulation of divine service in churches; questions of prize during war, and claims that arise out of accidents and shipwrecks at sea; adjudicate upon disputes relating to the form and validity of wills; and grant separations and divorces to married people.

Equity is a principle acting in conjunction with the law to soften and correct its operation in certain cases, by taking cognizance of those trusts and confidences which, although binding upon the conscience, a Court of Common Law is unable to enforce. For a long time after its introduction, Equity was a principle, separate, and sometimes antagonistic, to the law, and was administered in courts of its own, presided over by judges trained to its practice, assisted by advocates who made it a distinct profession. You can imagine, I dare say, without much difficulty, how questions both of Law and

Equity might be mixed up in one dispute, but it could not be decided by the tribunals of either acting separately. Thus, under the old system, if an estate were given to me *on trust*, to pay the rent and profits of it to your uncle, and to allow him quiet enjoyment of it, I should be considered, in the Common Law Courts on one side of Westminster Hall, the sole owner of the land, and might bring an action against him as a trespasser upon it; but in the Courts of Chancery, on the other side, he would be the real beneficiary owner, and I should be treated merely as the channel through which his property came. Again, if I had a patent invention which you unlawfully used, I could have obtained from an Equity judge, an injunction commanding you to cease from using it without my permission; but I should have had to bring an action at Common Law before I could recover damages against you for infringing my rights. So in the case which I put first, your uncle could not have pleaded in a Court of Law that I was merely a trustee for him, but as such, Equity would have restrained me from proceeding further in my action. Thus an appeal to two tribunals was frequently requisite to obtain redress for a single wrong, or to settle one and the same dispute.

Proceedings in Chancery were protracted and

expensive in the extreme. A suit sometimes lasted for twenty years, or longer still, and costs more than the value of the subject-matter of the dispute were frequently incurred. Every person interested to the most remote degree, whether in Law or Equity, was made a plaintiff or defendant as the case might be, and if any of them died, or, being a female, married, the suit *abated*, or ceased, and the proceedings had to be begun all over again.

These anomalies and stumbling-blocks in the path of justice no longer exist to the same extent as formerly. The principles of Equity are now, by recent legislation, acknowledged and acted upon in Courts of Common Law, and Common Law relief and compensation is in like manner granted by Courts of Chancery. The practice of equity has been rendered much more rapid and inexpensive, and suits do not abate as long as the parties or their representatives are qualified and willing to carry them on. In America, whose legal code is founded upon our own, Law and Equity are administered indifferently in the same courts, by the same judges, and are applied as the justice of the case demands. We are progressing, although not so rapidly as might be desired, towards an equally simple and desirable procedure.

The laws are interpreted and administered by the Judges in the courts I shall mention by-and-by, and their decisions are *executed* or enforced, in the name of the Sovereign, by the sheriffs of the various counties into which the kingdom is divided. The office of the sheriff—*shire reeve*, or *shire gereffa*—is of great antiquity; it is held for one year only at the nomination of the Crown. All arrests for debt are made by the officers of the sheriff, who is responsible for the safe custody of the debtor. He has also to summon juries to serve upon trials, and to carry out the extreme sentence of the criminal law. The powers which he exercises in the election of members of Parliament I have already sketched, and I will briefly notice those judicial functions which he has to perform, when I write to you about the proceedings in an action at law. As keeper of the Queen's peace in his county, the sheriff is the first man in it, not excepting the lord-lieutenant, who, as the successor of the *earl*, as I have told you already, was once its chief military governor. By virtue of his office the sheriff possesses the powers of a justice; but, being the executor of the law, he may not act as an ordinary magistrate in administering it. He is bound to defend his county against all the Queen's enemies, and must take into custody all traitors and felons; and to enable him to do so, may summon to his assistance all the people in the county under the rank of a peer. This is called the *posse comitatus,* or power of the county.

OFFICE OF SHERIFF. 147

Such are the duties and powers of the sheriff as defined by laws now in full force, but in *practice* he is hardly ever called upon to perform them. His deputy, the under-sheriff, transacts all the legal, judicial, and formal duties of the office; the police relieve him from the trouble of looking after criminals; and the time has passed in which our national defences could safely be trusted in his hands, however brave or loyal he may be. It is still a distinction to hold this post of high sheriff, as none but gentlemen of character and sufficient property are usually nominated to fill it. They have to accompany, and entertain the judges of assize through their county, and to provide a sufficient escort of javelin men for their protection. They sit on the right hand of the presiding judge at criminal trials, girt with a sword; and when there is a "maiden assize," that is one at which there are no prisoners to be tried, they present him with a pair of white gloves. When they have done this, and presided at any election that may take place during their years of office, they have done all that is required of them. So that when in future Letters I tell you that the sheriff has to do this or that, you will understand that his deputy, the under-sheriff, has to do it for him.

LETTER XIV.

THE COURTS OF LAW AND EQUITY, AND THEIR PROCEDURE.

The Superior Courts—Circuits of the Judges—Their several Commissions—District Courts of Record—Counsel and Attorney—The Inns of Court—An Action at Law—The Pleadings—The Jury—The Trial—The Verdict—Judgment by Default—The Costs—Execution—Judges in Equity.

A "COURT" is defined to be a place wherein justice is judicially administered. As the power of executing the laws is vested by our constitution in the Sovereign, it follows that all courts of justice derive their power from the Crown.

The principal courts of Common Law hold their sittings in Westminster Hall, and are three in number,—the Court of Queen's Bench, the Court of Common Pleas, and the Court of Exchequer. The judges of the two former are called *Justices*, those of the latter *Barons*. The Lord Chief Justice of England and four justices preside in the Court of Queen's Bench; the Chief Justice of the Common Pleas and the same number of justices sit in that court, and the Lord Chief Baron and four barons in the Court of Exchequer. These judges hold their offices for life, and can only be removed for misconduct upon a petition of both Houses of Parliament to the Crown. Formerly each of these courts had a separate jurisdiction: the King's Bench only heard criminal causes, and such as related to the controlling of inferior tribunals; the Common Pleas was for trials between subject and subject; and the Exchequer decided only such causes as related to the collection of the revenue. Now, however, these distinctions, long since evaded by legal fictions, are done away with by statute, and a private person may bring his action in any one of these courts. But the Queen's Bench still retains special jurisdiction in certain particulars; it keeps all inferior courts within the bounds of their authority, and may either order their proceedings to be removed for its own consideration, or may prohibit their progress altogether. It controls all civil corporations in the kingdom, it commands magistrates and others to do what the law requires in every case where there is no other course prescribed, and has both a criminal and civil jurisdiction.

Twice a year, in the spring and summer, the judges of these courts go round the whole country *on circuit*, to try actions at law, and criminals. The sittings which they hold in the principal town in each county are called *Assizes*.

England and Wales are divided into eight circuits, as follows:

THE HOME CIRCUIT:
> *Assize Towns*—Hertford, Chelmsford, Lewes, Maidstone, Croydon, Kingston and Guildford.

THE NORFOLK CIRCUIT:
> *Assize Towns*—Aylesbury, Bedford, Huntingdon, Cambridge, Norwich, Oakham, Leicester, Northampton, and Ipswich.

THE MIDLAND CIRCUIT:
> *Assize Towns*—York, Leeds, Nottingham, Lincoln, Derby, and Warwick.

THE OXFORD CIRCUIT:
> *Assize Towns*—Abingdon, Oxford, Worcester, Stafford, Shrewsbury, Hereford, Monmouth, and Gloucester.

THE WESTERN CIRCUIT:
> *Assize Towns*—Devizes, Winchester, Exeter, Dorchester, Bodmin, Wells, and Bristol.

THE NORTHERN CIRCUIT:
> *Assize Towns*—Durham, Newcastle, Carlisle, Appleby, Lancaster, Manchester, and Liverpool.

THE NORTH WALES CIRCUIT:
> *Assize Towns*—Newtown, Dolgelley, Carnarvon, Beaumaris, Ruthin, Mold, and Chester.

THE SOUTH WALES CIRCUIT:
> *Assize Towns*—Cardiff, Haverfordwest, Cardigan, Carmarthen, Brecon, Preston, and Chester, where the Welsh Circuits join.

Two judges go on each of these circuits, except

the last two, and in turn transact the civil and criminal business in its towns, except in the county palatine of Lancaster, in which the senior judge always presides in the criminal, or Crown, court. On the Welsh circuits only one judge attends, on account of the smallness of the business to be transacted.

In the more populous counties a *Winter Assize*, or Gaol Delivery, is held, for the trial of prisoners, and in a few instances the judges also take civil business at the same time.

The judges transact the business upon circuit by virtue of five separate authorities, only two of which I need mention here, in treating of civil procedure, namely, the commission of *assize*, authorizing them to hear and determine disputes relating to land, and the commission of *nisi prius*, which empowers them to try all actions pending in the superior courts that are ripe to be heard. These causes are appointed to be tried at Westminster, before a jury of the county out of which the dispute arose, *nisi prius (unless before)* the day fixed, the judges come into that county to hear and decide it.

There are also distinct Courts of Record, such as the Courts of Common Pleas of the counties of Durham and Lancaster, the Passage Court of Liverpool, and the Court of Record of Manchester, having the same procedure as the superior courts, and an unlimited, or limited jurisdiction, as to the amount they can award, according to their constitution.

Any person may bring, and defend, his own action in person, but almost all the business of our courts of law is carried on by counsel and attorneys, selected by the parties to act for them. The former are of two classes, *serjeants-at-law*, and *barristers*, some of whom are appointed Queen's counsel by patent from the Crown—all these fall under the general name of *Counsel*. From the most eminent of these the judges are selected. The Chief Justices and Chief Baron are appointed by the Prime Minister; the lesser, or *puisne* judges, by the Lord Chancellor. The privilege of calling persons to the bar to act as barristers in England is exclusively held by four ancient societies; viz., that of Lincoln's Inn, the Middle and Inner Temple, and Gray's Inn. Until recently students had only to pay some fees and to eat a certain number of dinners in the halls of these societies to entitle them to be *called to the bar;* but they have now to undergo a preliminary examination in general knowledge before they are admitted as students, and they must also pass an examination in law, or attend lectures instituted for their legal education, before they are granted the degree of barrister-at-law, which confers the liberty of practising in all English courts (except those in Doctors' Commons, in which those only who have taken the university degree of Doctor of Laws have audience as advocates), and gives a legal right to the title of *esquire*.

An attorney is one who is put in the place or *turn* of another to manage his affairs. Attorneys are now formed into a regular society, to which, in conjunction with some officials named by act of Parliament, the examination of persons desiring to become members of this profession, and the charge of the *rolls* or lists of persons duly entitled to practise in it, is confided. Once admitted and sworn, an attorney may practise in any court except the Court of Chancery, to act in which he must be admitted a *Solicitor* thereof. Persons are *admitted* by the superior courts after they have served for a certain time as clerks in the office of an attorney or solicitor, under a legal instrument called *articles of clerkship*, and have passed an examination in law. They are then considered to be officers of the courts. The judges exercise strict supervision over their conduct, and may strike their names off the rolls, should it be proved to their satisfaction that they have been guilty of conduct deserving such a punishment. Attorneys and solicitors have to take out a *certificate* every year, upon which they have to pay a fee for leave to pursue their vocation.

The actions most commonly brought in the courts of Common Law are to recover disputed debts or demands, the possession of land, or a compensation in money called *damages*, for acts committed or neglected to be done whereby the plaintiff suffers an injury in his person, property, or reputation.

When an action is to be brought, the plaintiff lays his case before an attorney, who issues a writ summoning the defendant to *appear* to answer the complaint of the plaintiff. This "appearance" is made by his lodging with the proper officer of the court, a writing stating where notices and further proceedings may be served upon him. The next step is the delivery by the plaintiff of a statement in writing of his cause of action, called the *declaration*. The defendant's answer to this is called the *plea;* this is also in writing. Parties may now bring both the law, and the facts of their cases into question. Formerly, by disputing the one, they were held to admit the other, and thus great injustice was frequently done. The declaration and plea form part of what is called the *pleadings* in an action, the objects of which are to ascertain what is really in controversy between the parties, so as to exclude all that is immaterial or irrelevant. Thus the plaintiff having stated facts constituting his cause of action, the defendant is obliged to deny them, or, confessing their accuracy, to avoid their effect by asserting fresh ones, or, admitting them, to deny the legal effect contended for by the plaintiff. The plaintiff then *replies* in like manner, and the defendant *rejoins*, until some fact is asserted on the one side, and denied on the other, or some proposition of law is relied upon by the one, and disputed by the other. The questions thus raised are *issues* in fact or law, according to circumstances. The latter are argued before the judges of the court in which the action is brought, and decided by them; the former go before a *jury*.

The pleadings on either side, and the issues *joined*—that is accepted as the matter in dispute by the parties, form the *record* of the action.

All natural born subjects between the ages of twenty-one and sixty, who have an income of 10*l*. from land or tenements of freehold, or 20*l*. from leaseholds, or, being householders, are rated to the poor at 30*l*., are qualified to be *jurors*. In Wales the qualification is one-fifth less than above; but in the city of London no man can serve upon a jury who is not a householder, or occupier of a shop or counting-house, and worth 100*l*. a year. A book called the *Jurors' Book* is kept by the sheriff, in which is entered the names of all qualified persons, and from this he selects the *panel*, or list, which, in obedience to the writ *venire facias juratores*, he sends to the sittings, or assizes, and summons those persons included in it to attend there under pain of a penalty of not less than forty shillings. They receive no remuneration for their services. Thus is formed the *common jury*.

If either plaintiff or defendant wish to have their case tried before a higher class than this, they may demand a *special jury*. The special jury list, kept as before by the sheriff, contains the names of more wealthy persons than the common jury. They are selected and summoned in the same way, and paid one guinea a-piece by the party who required their services, unless the judge orders otherwise.

The following persons are exempted from serving on juries:—Peers, judges, clergymen of all denominations acknowledged by law, doctors of laws, advocates, barristers and solicitors in practice, officers of the army and navy, of courts of law and equity, and of the customs and excise, physicians and surgeons, pilots, persons engaged in laying down buoys for the Trinity House, the household of the Sovereign, sheriffs' officers, parish clerks, and all persons above sixty years of age.

When a cause is ripe for trial, the attorneys for either party make out statements of the facts and circumstances of their cases in writing, which are called *briefs*. They then generally select a queen's counsel or serjeant to conduct the case, and one or more barristers to assist them, giving each a brief, upon which is marked the fee by which they propose to reward these services. The fee of a barrister and a physician, is considered in the light of a free gift, or *honorarium*, which cannot be demanded or recovered at law.

A jury of twelve householders is then empanelled as follows: The names of all the jurors summoned are written each upon a separate piece of paper and put into a box; the officer of the court selects twelve at random, and these form the jury. The judge having taken his seat, and the jury sworn to give a true verdict between the parties, the trial commences. The junior counsel for the plaintiff *opens the pleadings*, stating the *issue* to be tried; the *leading* or senior counsel then states the facts of the case to the jury, after which the witnesses, by whose testimony it is to be supported, are examined by the counsel for the plaintiff, generally in turn—this is called the *examination in chief*. The defendant's counsel may then *cross-examine* the witnesses as they are called forward, to test the truth of their story, and require them to answer as to such other circumstances as may favour the defendant's

unliquidated damages, or damages the extent of which have yet to be ascertained, are sought, the plaintiff has to call upon the sheriff to *assess* the damages. The sheriff summons a jury, and holds his court (which is generally presided over by his deputy); the plaintiff proves his case, and the defendant may be heard in reduction of damages. The jury fix what sum is to be paid, and it is recovered according to law. If the defendant refuses or neglects to pay in this, as in any other case in which a verdict or judgment is given against him, his property may be seized by the sheriff under a writ from the court, and sold to raise the required sum, or he may be arrested and imprisoned until he shall have satisfied it, if he has the means of so doing.

The parties may agree to accept the opinion of a judge upon the law and the facts of their case, and when his decision is given, it has all the force of a verdict by a jury. Actions involving mere questions of account, are often referred to some competent person, whose *award* is made a rule of court, and enforced by it.

If the question in dispute be an abstract point of law, the parties may state it for decision to the court in what is called a *special case,* without pleadings.

THE JUDGES IN EQUITY. 161

The costs of the suit are generally paid by the party against whom a decision or verdict is ultimately given, but if an action, which might have been brought in a county court, is brought in the superior courts for a debt under 20*l*., the plaintiff will not get his costs, unless the judge certifies that it was a proper case to be brought there for trial. If it is brought to recover compensation for a wrong —in legal language a *tort*—he must obtain a verdict for 5*l*. to entitle him to costs.

In the local Courts of Record, a verdict of forty shillings generally entitles the plaintiff to his costs.

In addition to the sittings held in Westminster Hall, in the district Courts of Record, and at the Assizes for the trial of actions, there are the new *County Courts*, which, with a very simple procedure, decide cases in which the sum in dispute does not exceed 50*l*.; but, with the consent of the suitors, an action to any amount, but not of any character, may be tried there. The judge usually decides both upon the law and the facts of the case, unless either of the parties desire to have it tried before a jury, which in these courts consists of five persons.

Such is the legal jurisdiction of the county courts; and by an Act passed in the present year (1865) an equitable jurisdiction has also been conferred upon them. That jurisdiction is given in all suits by creditors, legatees, devisees, heirs-at-law, or next-of-kin, against or for an account of administration of property not exceeding 500*l.* in value; in suits for the execution of trusts, the property not exceeding 500*l.*; in suits for foreclosure or redemption or enforcing a charge, the property not exceeding 500*l.*; in suits for the dissolution or winding-up of partnership, the partnership assets not exceeding 500*l.*; and in some other cases with a like restriction as to amount. A Vice-Chancellor sitting at chambers has, however, the power to make an order transferring the suit to the Court of Chancery.

The judges in Equity are the Lord Chancellor, two Lords Justices of Appeal, the Master of the Rolls, and three Vice-Chancellors. Appeals from the decisions of the four latter are heard, first, before the Lords Justices, or the Lord Chancellor, and then before the House of Lords. The Lord Chancellor has the appointment of all Justices of the Peace, in the name of the Crown. He is the Keeper of the Great Seal and of the Sovereign's conscience—the office having been formerly held by an ecclesiastic. He is the patron of all livings in the Church in the gift of the Queen under a certain value; he is the guardian of all infants (as persons under the age of twenty-one years are

COURT OF BANKRUPTCY. 163

called in law), idiots, and lunatics, and has the general control over all charitable trusts.

The Master of the Rolls is the only Equity judge who may sit in the House of Commons.

Proceedings in the Courts of *Equity* are commenced by *bill, claim,* or *petition:* these are written pleadings, in which the plaintiff states his complaint and prays a remedy. Should questions of *fact* arise in a Chancery suit, the judge may direct the *issue* to be tried before a Court of Common Law. Cases relating to the interpretation of deeds of settlement and other legal instruments, the execution of trusts, the granting of injunctions, &c. &c., are those which come, commonly, before Courts of Equity.

The Courts of Bankruptcy administer the law for the protection of unfortunate traders and other persons unable to pay their debts, and for securing to their creditors an equal distribution of their possessions, called their *estate.* It is now considered worse than useless to lock up an insolvent debtor in prison, (unless it be by way of punishment for dishonest dealing,) when, if free, he might be earning money to pay his liabilities.

When the bankrupt has conformed to the law by making a perfect disclosure of his affairs, if his conduct has not been grossly culpable, he obtains an order of discharge, which frees him from all personal liability as to his former debts, unless the court annexes to such discharge conditions requiring him to set apart a portion of his future earnings for the benefit of his creditors. The judges in Bankruptcy are called *Commissioners*, and rank with those of the superior courts. Three of them hold sittings in London, and in several large provincial towns there is a local court of bankruptcy, and one or two commissioners. An appeal from their courts lies to the Lords Justices, and from them to the House of Lords.

LETTER XV.

OF CRIMES AND OFFENCES.

Definition of Crimes—Treasons—Felonies—Misdemeanours—Punishments—Costs of Prosecutions—Accessaries and Accomplices—Nuisances—Common Law Offences.

BEFORE I enumerate to you the courts of criminal law and describe their procedure, I will briefly state over what sort of cases they have jurisdiction.

Crimes and offences are acts done, or omitted, in violation of some public law. It is the duty of the head of a State to prevent their commission as far as possible, and to inflict suitable punishment upon those who are proved to have taken part in them; not from a feeling of revenge against the evil-doers, but to make of them examples to deter others from similarly offending.

Offences against the criminal law are divided under three heads: *treasons, felonies,* and *misdemeanours.* The two latter together represent again two divisions of offences—1st, those acts evil in themselves (*mala in se*) forbidden from the first by the revealed law of God, such as murder, theft, and other crimes; and 2nd, those which the spread of civilization has required mankind to provide against (*mala prohibita*), such as coining false money, frauds on the revenue, tampering with signals on railways, &c.

The principal crimes known to the laws, into which it is fit that we should enquire, are as follow:—

High Treason.—This crime now comprises the "compassing, contriving, inventing, or intending death or destruction, or any bodily harm tending to death or destruction; or wounding, imprisonment, or restraint of the heirs and successors of his Majesty King George the Third;" in "levying war against the Sovereign within the realm," and in "adhering to her enemies, giving them aid or comfort in the realm or elsewhere." All the other offences made high treason by ancient statutes, such as imitating the Royal Sign Manual or the Great Seal, coining false money, &c., now rank as felonies, punishable by imprisonment and penal servitude.

The punishment for high treason is death; the law enacts that the person convicted "shall be drawn on a hurdle to the place of execution, and be then hanged by the neck until such person be dead, and that afterwards the head shall be severed from the body of such person, and the body divided into four quarters, shall be disposed of as his Majesty King George the Third and his successors shall think fit." The sovereign, "by warrant under the sign manual counter-signed by a secretary of state, may direct that the offender shall not be drawn, but shall be taken in such a manner as in the warrant shall be expressed, to the place of execution, and that he shall not be there hanged by the neck, but that instead thereof the head shall be there severed from the body whilst alive, and in such warrant direction may be given as to, and in, what manner the body, head, and quarters shall be disposed of." Barbarous and disgusting as these details appear, the ancient punishment for high treason was more revolting still.

Murder is the taking away of the life of a fellow-creature intentionally, and with *malice*. The punishment for murder is death by hanging.

Manslaughter is the taking away of the life of a fellow-creature *un*intentionally, by accident, or in sudden anger, *without malice*. Slaying a person in self defence is not a crime. As the offence of manslaughter ranges from something very nearly akin to murder, down to mere mischance, to which hardly any blame attaches, so the punishment for it varies from penal servitude for life, down to a nominal imprisonment, according to the circumstances of the case.

Attempting to murder by shooting, poisoning, stabbing, &c. These crimes were formerly *capital*, that is, they were punishable with death, but under the Criminal Statutes Consolidation Acts of 1861, the punishment was reduced to penal servitude, which may, however, extend to the period of the culprit's natural life.

Stabbing, shooting, or throwing explosive or corrosive substances upon any person, with intent to disable, maim, or disfigure, or do some grievous bodily harm. Punishment—penal servitude, or imprisonment with hard labour.

Robbery—Stealing from the person with violence, or threats of violence. It is punishable by penal servitude or imprisonment.

Burglary—Breaking into a dwelling-house between the hours of nine at night and six in the morning, with intent to steal therein; or (*having committed a felony, or being in a house with the intention* of committing one) breaking *out* of it between the same hours. It is not necessary that the premises should be actually damaged to constitute this offence. Opening a door or a window that has been closed, is a constructive " breaking" in the eyes of the law. Punishment—penal servitude or imprisonment with hard labour.

Housebreaking—The same offence committed in the day-time. Punishment—penal servitude, or imprisonment with hard labour.

Forgery—Making false bank notes, cheques, signatures, wills, &c., or altering part of a genuine instrument with intent to defraud. Punishment as above.

Uttering the above—that is, attempting to pass them off as genuine, knowing them to be false and counterfeit. Punishment as above.

Bigamy—Marrying again in the lifetime of a wife or husband. Punishment as above.

Piracy—Seizing, and stealing from, ships at sea; punishable by penal servitude and imprisonment with hard labour.

Arson—Setting fire to houses, buildings, stacks, ships, &c. Punishment—imprisonment with hard labour, or penal servitude. If a person or persons be in the house at the time it is set on fire, the incendiary may be sentenced to penal servitude for life.

Coining—Making false money. Punishment—penal servitude or imprisonment with hard labour.

Larceny—Stealing. When committed by clerks or servants, or from a dwelling-house to the value of 5*l.*, and in some other cases, penal servitude may be awarded; but unless a previous conviction for another felony be proved against the thief, imprisonment with hard labour is the usual punishment.

Receiving stolen goods, knowing them to have been stolen. Punishment as above.

Embezzlement—The wrongful appropriation by clerks and servants of money or property received by them, by virtue of their employment as such for their master. Punishment—penal servitude, or imprisonment with hard labour.

Rioting—Rioters are punishable by imprisonment with hard labour; or with penal servitude, if they remain together after being called upon by a magistrate to disperse.

Escaping from prison. Imprisonment or penal servitude, according to the offence for which the prisoner was in confinement.

Returning from transportation. Same punishment.

Assisting a prisoner to escape, with many other offences, are *felonies.* The following are misdemeanours:—

Perjury—Taking a false oath. Punishment—penal servitude, or imprisonment with hard labour.

Cheating—Obtaining money or goods by false pretences, or fraud. Punishment—penal servitude, or imprisonment with hard labour.

Assaults—Unlawful attacks upon the person,

without the intents before mentioned. Punishment—fine, or imprisonment with or without hard labour.

Conspiracy—Two or more persons combining together for an unlawful purpose, or to carry out a lawful one by *un*lawful means. Punishment—fine, or imprisonment with or without hard labour.

Uttering, or passing base or false coin. Punishment—imprisonment with hard labour; after previous conviction, penal servitude.

Publishing libels against individuals, or blasphemous or seditious statements against religion or government. Punishment—fine, or imprisonment, or both.

Poaching—Trespassing in pursuit, and destruction of game; punishable, according to the time and manner in which it is committed, and the number of persons engaged together, by penal servitude, or imprisonment with hard labour.

Gambling—Using false scales and weights—Smuggling—Sending threatening letters, &c. &c. —are misdemeanours punishable variously, by fine, imprisonment, and penal servitude.

Finally, all *attempts* to commit felonies are misdemeanours. The amount of punishment to be awarded is within certain limits, which I need not lay down, in the discretion of the judge. Not more than two years' imprisonment can generally be given, but penal servitude for life, or any lesser term, can be awarded for serious offences. The punishment of transportation is now abolished, as our colonies are no longer willing to receive convicts, but criminals sentenced to penal servitude may be sent abroad wherever her Majesty, through her Secretary of State, may direct.

The above misdemeanours are of a *public* nature, affecting the peace and prosperity of the country, and the honour of its government. In some of them, such as assaults and libels, a double remedy is open to the injured person; he may put the criminal law in motion against his assailant, and have him punished for offending against the law and breaking the peace, and he may bring a civil action against him, and obtain damages for the private wrong done to his person or character. As a general rule it is however advisable to take only one of these courses, as it is not likely that a jury would give heavy damages against a man who had already suffered punishment, or that a judge would pass a severe sentence upon a man who had already been made to pay largely for committing the same offence. But there are cases in which both civil and criminal remedies may very properly be taken, the one to compensate an injured individual, the other to vindicate an outraged law.

The cost of prosecuting persons for having committed any of the misdemeanours or felonies above enumerated, and others which have not been mentioned, is paid by the State out of the Consolidated Fund, whether the prisoner be *convicted,* that is, proved to be guilty, or acquitted.

Persons who combine together for the purpose of committing any offence and act in concert are all equally guilty. Thus, if several men conspire to rob a house, and some of them watch outside to prevent surprise, whilst one of their number commits a felony within, they are each and all guilty of his crime. Persons so assisting are *principals in the second degree.*

Accessaries before the fact are such as command or procure a felony to be committed. Those who harbour or assist the principal felon, by hiding him, or providing him with money or a horse, &c. &c., to escape, are *accessaries after the fact.* Either class may be tried with the principal felon, or by themselves, even although he may not have been brought to trial. But his crime must be proved to have been committed.

Ignorance of the law will not excuse from the consequences of guilt, any one who has capacity to understand it. All persons are presumed to know the law, but infants under the age of seven years are supposed to be incapable of committing a capital offence; and from that age up to fourteen it must appear that they know right from wrong before the law will be put in force to punish them.

Persons of unsound mind are also exempted from punishment, as also are those who act in subjection to the powers of another, for neither can be said to have a will of their own. But the frenzy and temporary insanity produced by drunkenness is no excuse; for this is the consequence of a vice voluntarily indulged in, and not, as in the case of lunacy and madness, the act of God, which no man can prevent.

A married woman who commits a felony (other than murder) jointly with her husband, in his presence, and with his sanction, cannot be convicted, for, in contemplation of law, she always acts under his control. Neither can she be convicted of stealing his goods, for in the eye of the law husband and wife are one; but if she steals them to give to an adulterer, the latter may be convicted if he carries them off or takes possession of them, well knowing at the time that they have been stolen by his paramour from her husband.

There are numerous misdemeanours of a *private* nature affecting the rights of individuals or societies, such as committing or maintaining *nuisances* prejudicial to the health of a man, or of the dis-

COMMON LAW OFFENCES. 175

trict in which he lives (such as chemical works), or to his or their repose and morality (such as disorderly gatherings), or to his or their peace of mind (such as keeping large stores of inflammable or explosive substances likely to create a conflagration, &c.), the expenses of prosecuting which must be borne by the parties complaining.

Persons or corporate bodies whose duty it is to make or keep in repair roads, bridges, or buildings, may be indicted for a misdemeanour if they refuse or neglect to do so.

You must understand, however, that although most of the crimes that can be committed are defined and forbidden by act of Parliament, still a remedy exists at common law for many offences against public justice, peace, or morality, that may not come within the strict letter of any statute; but no *new* offence can be dealt with under the common law, because, as I have said, it consists only of ancient customs. When a remedy has been provided, or a course of prosecution pointed out, by a statute, the common law yields to it. All statutes which impose penalties must be construed most strongly *against* the Crown and in favour of the subject. No person may be tried or punished twice for the same offence; if it is attempted to do so, he may plead *autrefois convict* (before convicted) or *autrefois acquit* (before acquitted) to the indictment.

LETTER XVI.

OF THE COURTS OF CRIMINAL LAW.

The High Court of Parliament—The Court of the Lord High Steward—The Queen's Bench—Office of Coroner—Of Justices of the Peace—The Assize Courts—The Central Criminal Court —Quarter and Petty Sessions—Jurisdiction of Justices of the Peace and Police Magistrates.

Now that you know the nature of many of the offences that are punishable by our laws, I will show you by what tribunals persons suspected of having committed them are tried.

In the letter in which I described the constitution of Parliament, I told you that the House of Lords has the right of trying persons impeached by the House of Commons. It has also the privilege, whilst Parliament is sitting, of trying its own members for treason or felony, but not for misdemeanours. A peer accused of any of these offences is tried in the ordinary way before a jury. A bishop, although he sits in the House of Lords, must be tried as a commoner. When Parliament is not sitting, peers may be tried for treason or felony in the courts of the Lord High Steward of England. This office is of great antiquity but is not filled now, except upon special occasions, such as the trial of a peer, for which a person is specially appointed to hold it, and when the business is over he breaks his wand of office and his functions are at an end. Trials in this court are held before not less than twenty-four peers, including the Lord High Steward, who is the judge. In trials before the Lords in Parliament, a High Steward is also appointed, not as judge, but as a kind of speaker to regulate the procedure.

The Sovereign is supposed to be the judge in these cases, and a majority of peers return the verdict of *guilty* or *not guilty*, not upon oath, but in the words, "*upon my honour.*"

The Court of Queen's Bench, besides its civil has a very important criminal jurisdiction. Practically speaking, it is the principal court of criminal jurisdiction in the country, and takes cognisance of all offences from high treason down to the most trivial assault. Indictments and other criminal proceedings from all the inferior courts may be removed into it, tried before its judges, and, if informal or illegal, set aside by them.

The Lord Chief Justice is the principal coroner of the kingdom, and all its judges are coroners and justices of the peace. It may be convenient here to state how coroners and justices of the peace are appointed, and what duties they have to perform.

The office of coroner is one of great antiquity and importance. The coroner is elected by the freeholders of the county or district within which he holds his court, and his principal duty is to enquire, with a jury, into the circumstances attending every sudden death. This proceeding is called an *inquest*, and in strictness should be held in sight of the body of the departed person, but this rule has been very much relaxed. It is now customary for the coroner and jury to view the body, and then to adjourn to some convenient place to hear the evidence, and to draw up the *inquisition* or *finding*, as to how the death was caused. If the body cannot be found, there can be no coroner's inquisition, and the inquiry must be conducted by justices of the peace.

Should it turn out that murder or manslaughter has been committed, it is the duty of the coroner to commit the suspected person or persons for trial, and the inquisition, which must be signed by him and twelve of the jury, has all the force of a bill of indictment that has been "found" by the grand jury—a proceeding which I will explain hereafter. The coroner is the deputy of the sheriff,

JUSTICES OF THE PEACE. 179

and when the law has to be executed against that officer, the coroner must execute it.

Justices of the peace are gentlemen appointed by the special commission of the Sovereign, at the recommendation of the Lord Lieutenant of their county, to assist in the administration of the law in some cases. They must have a qualification of the value of 100*l.* a year, arising out of landed estate. Certain persons, however, such as justices of corporations, peers, privy councillors, judges, and others, are privileged to act without such qualification. Their duty is to preserve the Queen's peace by committing to prison any person actually guilty of a breach of the peace, and to bind over to be of good behaviour such as are suspected of being about to become so; also to prevent and suppress riots and affrays, by apprehending disorderly persons; and they have to administer the law at general and petty sessions, as will be seen hereafter. They discharge these services without any fee or salary.

The courts of *Oyer* and *Terminer* and *general gaol delivery* are those which are held upon circuit in every county, before the judges of assize, and commissioners appointed to assist them.

It has already been stated that the judges and commissioners of assize sit under five distinct commissions; two of these, which relate to the discharge of their civil jurisdiction, have already been described. The remaining three give them power to act in criminal cases, and are—3rd, *the commission of the peace;* 4th, of *oyer* and *terminer;* and 5th, *general gaol delivery.* The duty of a justice of the peace has been lately laid down. The commission of *oyer* and *terminer* authorises the persons named in it to enquire, hear, and determine all treasons, felonies, and misdemeanours; and that of *general gaol delivery* to try and deliver every prisoner who shall be in the gaol when the judges arrive at the circuit town, no matter by whom they are indicted, or of what crime they are charged.

The Central Criminal Court has jurisdiction to try all offences committed in London and Middlesex, and in certain parts of Essex, Kent, and Surrey adjoining. This court sits once a month, and is presided over by the Recorder, and Common Sergeant, of the City of London; by a third commissioner—generally the judge of the sheriffs' court; and by her Majesty's judges of the superior courts, two, or more, of whom attend in rotation and try the more serious offences. If it be proved that a person is not likely to obtain a fair trial in the county in which the crime was committed, he may be removed for trial into this court. He may be also tried "at bar," before the judges of the Queen's Bench.

The Assize Courts, Central Criminal Court, and Court of Queen's Bench, have power to try all treasons, felonies, and misdemeanours, committed or removed for trial within their jurisdiction.

The courts of quarter sessions of the peace have a limited jurisdiction. They are restrained from trying all capital offences, and many others. Thieving, unaccompanied with violence; obtaining money or valuables under false pretences; attempts to commit felonies, indictments against nuisances, and for the non-performance of public duties; offences relating to game, highways, alehouses; the settlement and provision for the poor; disputes between masters, their apprentices, and servants, are the class of cases usually heard and decided before them.

The courts of quarter sessions in counties are held before the justices of the peace, whose chairman presides. In some populous counties a barrister of standing and experience is appointed to that post by the justices, and receives a salary for his services. In cities and boroughs the Recorder is the judge. As their name implies, these courts are held quarterly, but in places where the business to be transacted is considerable, they sit by adjournment at intervening periods.

Lastly, we have the courts of petty sessions, which, in country places, are held before two or more justices of the peace, and in populous towns are presided over by a stipendiary magistrate, who must be a barrister of a certain standing, and who receives a salary for his services. The first proceeding in all criminal cases, except high treason, takes place in these courts. They have power to deal with many cases of a trivial nature summarily—that is, to dispose of them by punishing or discharging the accused upon their own responsibility. The graver class of criminals they commit for trial, to the assizes or the sessions, according to the nature of the charge made against them. Persons suspected of high treason are generally examined before a Secretary of State, and committed for trial or discharged by him.

It is not necessary to trouble you with the constitution and practice of other courts of a criminal jurisdiction, which are seldom resorted to. My object has been to give you a concise and practical view of the machinery of our criminal law, and this is comprised, to all useful intents and purposes, in the courts which I have mentioned.

LETTER XVII.

OF THE PRACTICE OF THE CRIMINAL LAW.

Conduct of Public Prosecutions—Arrest of Prisoners by the Police—Examination before Magistrates—Committal or Discharge of Prisoners—Indictments—Office of the Grand Jury—Trial—Challenges of Jurors—Proceedings at Trial—Court of Criminal Appeal—Pardons.

WE have no official charged to institute and conduct the legal proceedings against suspected persons. Most continental states have a *Public Prosecutor* appointed by government, and charged to put the criminal law in operation; and very many persons are of opinion that we ought to have such a functionary in England. It is urged that we have no security that every offender is brought to justice; and that some may escape, owing to the proper steps not being taken for their apprehension. Further, that others, by intimidation and bribes, may induce the persons they have injured to defeat justice by absenting themselves at the trial. The trial itself too, may be conducted in such a slovenly manner as to result in a verdict of acquittal. There is much truth in this; but I am by no means sure that the appointment of a public prosecutor would lessen the occurrence of these possible evils. When once information is given of the commission of a crime, he is a clever man, indeed, who can elude for any length of time the vigilance and perseverance of our detective police. No public prosecutor could prevent a witness being bribed; and as to the conducting of cases in court, I think that as our bar is constituted —every man vying with his fellow for practice, and striving to distinguish himself—it may be better relied upon for properly managing criminal prosecutions, than any set of officials secure of a position and its stipend. In every town where there is a bench of magistrates, there are attorneys who act as their clerks, and get up the evidence against persons committed for trial, and instruct counsel to prosecute. They are paid according to the number of cases entrusted to them, and it is to their interest, of course, that every complaint should be investigated. In large towns, such as Manchester, Liverpool, Birmingham, &c., there is an attorney specially appointed by the corporation to attend to all prosecutions. These are, in point of fact, public prosecutors, and, as far as I can judge, no reflection can be cast upon the way in which they manage their business, or select counsel to conduct it.

In the first instance, the police are practically public prosecutors. They apprehend persons in the commission of crime, receive information of offences that have been done in secret, and collect evidence.

Justice, whether it be in criminal or civil cases, is administered in public, and the latter always in presence of the accused parties. A prisoner must be brought before a magistrate upon the earliest opportunity after his capture. The evidence tendered against him is heard, taken down in writing, and signed by the witness who gives it. This is called his *deposition*, and the prisoner, if committed for trial, has an absolute right to a copy of this on paying a small fee for making it out. If the evidence is not complete at the first hearing, but enough is given to raise a strong presumption against the prisoner, the magistrate has the power of "remanding" him, or sending him back to prison for eight days, whilst further proofs are being collected, or of taking "bail" for his appearance to answer the charge. To be admitted to bail, a prisoner must get two or more householders, to be bound to bring him forward when required, on pain of incurring a penalty, fixed by the magistrate, in case they should fail to do so. Sometimes the prisoner's promise, under a penalty, to appear, is taken as sufficient. When all the evidence that can be obtained is collected, the accused is either summarily convicted and sentenced, or committed for trial to the assizes or sessions, where the witnesses and nominal prosecutor are bound over to appear against him; but when the evidence is insufficient to substantiate the charge against him, the prisoner is discharged. After committal for trial, the depositions are sent to the proper officer of the court in which the prisoner is to be tried, and there the "indictment" is prepared and written upon parchment. The indictment is a statement in legal language of the offence for which he has to answer, and in former days much exactness and technicality were required in its wording. The slightest error in stating the offence alleged, or the name or surname of the prisoner or prosecutor, or in describing the property stolen, was sufficient to render it invalid, and the prisoner escaped. Recent alterations in the law, however, have made it much more simple, and any mistakes, such as are not calculated to mislead the accused, or prejudice him in his defence, may be amended by order of the court. The proceedings in trials at assizes and sessions are almost identically the same.

The day for holding them having arrived, a grand and a petty jury are summoned by the sheriff of the county exactly as in civil cases; the jury for criminal and civil trials being taken indifferently from the same panel. But if a foreigner is to be tried, he is entitled to demand a jury *de medietate linguæ*, composed half of Englishmen and half of foreigners (not necessarily his own countrymen), whom the sheriff must summon. The indictments are laid before the *grand jury*, which consists usually of thirty persons, selected from amongst the magistrates and principal gentry in the county, who possess the qualification required of a justice of the peace. They examine only the witnesses in support of the charges against the prisoner to see if there be a sufficient ground to justify his being put upon his trial. If a majority of twelve agree that there is one, their *foreman*, the principal person on the jury, writes "a true bill" upon the indictment. If, on the contrary, no sufficiently strong case appears, he writes "no true bill" upon it, and in some counties cuts it across, and the prisoner is entitled to be liberated if there be no other charge against him. All the indictments are brought by the grand jury from the room in which they discharge their duties into open court, and there their decisions of "true" and "no true bill" on each is read out. Those prisoners against whom true bills are returned are then assembled in the dock, the indictment is read over to each by the officer of the court, and he is asked if he pleads "guilty" or "not guilty" to the charge. This is called "arraigning" the prisoners. Those who plead "guilty" have sentence passed upon them at once, and those who plead "not guilty" are brought up in turn to be tried before the petty jury.

Formerly if a prisoner refused to plead he was sentenced to endure *penance*, or the *peine forte et dure*. He was taken into the prison, laid upon his back in a low, dark chamber, and weights of iron as heavy as he could bear, were placed upon his chest. He was allowed for food three morsels of the worst bread upon the first day, and three draughts of the stagnant water that was nearest the prison door upon the second. Thus his daily sustenance was alternated, and thus he was kept, the weights upon his body being increased every day, until he *died*, or (as the ancient judgment ran) till he *answered*. It was only by the statute 12 Geo. III. c. 20, that this barbarity was put an end to.

Now, if a prisoner refuses to plead, a jury is impannelled to try whether he stands "*mute of malice*," or "*by the visitation of God*"—that is, if he be merely vexatiously silent, or incapable of answering by reason of being deaf, or dumb, or of unsound mind. If a verdict to the former effect is returned, a plea of "not guilty" is entered for him, and the trial proceeds; if the latter, the trial is postponed, and the prisoner sent to some asylum, from whence, should he recover his senses, he may be brought up again and tried.

It is not absolutely necessary that an accused person should be brought before a magistrate and committed before he can be indicted, although that is the most ordinary and proper course. An indictment may be preferred without his knowledge, and a "Bench Warrant" for his apprehension may be obtained from the presiding judge at assizes or sessions. By this means he loses the fair advantage which the law allows, in giving prisoners a copy of the depositions of the witnesses about to be examined against them; consequently it is a course which should not be adopted except upon extreme occasions, and one which has always of late years found disfavour with our judges, as being a proceeding by means of which the law may be employed by designing individuals as an engine of extortion or revenge.

An ordinary indictment for stealing is in the following form :

* *Kent,* to wit—

"*The jurors for our Lady the Queen upon their oath present that John Smith* (the prisoner), *on the first day of May, in the year of our Lord one thousand eight hundred and fifty-eight, one gold ring and one box of the goods and chattels of James Brown, feloniously did steal, take and carry away against the peace of our Lady the Queen, her crown and dignity.*"

Any number of prisoners may be charged in one indictment with an offence in which they have all been participators. Only one felony may be charged in one indictment—that is to say, you cannot indict a man for murder and burglary at once; but any number of misdemeanours may be included, and any number of indictments for distinct felonies may be brought in against one prisoner; and three acts of stealing, if committed within six months, from the first to the last, may be charged in the same indictment.

Persons may also be tried, as we have seen, upon a coroner's inquisition, without the intervention of a grand jury; and likewise upon an instru-

---

* Or whatever the county in which the offence was committed happens to be.

ment filed by the Attorney-General, called an *ex officio* information, and upon an information filed by the Master of the Crown Office. The former process has fallen into disuse and is seldom employed; the latter lies only for misdemeanours, and the accused person is always given an opportunity of showing cause why it should not be issued against him. Informations of either sort are tried in the Queen's Bench.

When a convenient number of prisoners have pleaded, the officer of the court addresses them thus:—

> "*Prisoners, these good men that you shall now hear called are the jurors who are to pass between our Sovereign Lady the Queen and you upon your trials; if, therefore, you, or either of you, will challenge them, or either of them, you must challenge them as they come to the book to be sworn, and before they are sworn, and you shall be heard.*"

The officer then proceeds to call twelve jurors from the list of those summoned, called the "panel," calling each juror by name and address. The jury then stand up in the jury-box, and are sworn one by one, and before the oath is administered, the prisoner may "challenge" or object to the serving upon his trial of any person there present.

Challenges are of two kinds—1st, to the *array*, when exception is taken to the whole number impannelled; and 2ndly, to the *polls*, when individual jurymen are objected to. They are divided again into challenges *peremptory*, for which no cause is stated, and *per causam*, when a reason is given. Both kinds of challenge may be made either on behalf of the Crown or the person about to be tried. For high treason thirty-five peremptory challenges may be made; in all other felonies the limit is twenty. In cases of misdemeanours there is no peremptory challenge. If the panel be exhausted by challenges of the prisoner and the Crown, or either, before a full jury has been obtained, the practice is to call over the whole panel again, but omitting those peremptorily challenged, and then, as each juror again appears, whichever party challenges must show cause for his objection.

Challenges for cause are either to the "array" or to individual jurymen. To the array, if the sheriff be supposed to have made an unjust panel; to the individual, when he is supposed to be actuated by ill-feeling or favour towards the prisoner whom he is to try. If the cause be disputed, two *triers* are appointed, who hear the evidence and decide upon oath whether the panel is improper, or the juror impartial.

When a full jury have been sworn, if the trial takes place at the assizes or the Central Criminal Court, the crier makes proclamation in the following form :—

> "*If any one can inform my lords the Queen's Justices, the Queen's Attorney-General, or the Queen's Sergeant, ere this inquest be taken between our Sovereign Lady the Queen and the prisoners at the bar, of any treasons, murder, felony, or misdemeanours, committed or done by them, or any of them, let him come forth and he shall be heard, for the prisoners stand at the bar upon their deliverance. God save the Queen.*"

The officer of the court then calls the prisoner about to be tried to the bar, and says :—

> "*Gentlemen of the jury, the prisoner stands indicted by the name of A. B., for that he* [and so on, stating an abstract of the indictment, to the end]; *upon this indictment he has been arraigned, and upon this arraignment he has pleaded that he is not guilty, and so for trial has put*

himself upon his country, which country you are. Your charge, therefore, is to inquire whether he be guilty or not guilty, and to hearken to the evidence."

This is called "giving the prisoner in charge to the jury."

The trial then commences. The counsel for the prosecution states the case against the accused to the jury, and calls the witnesses to support it. The prisoner, or his counsel, if he has one, may cross-examine them, and at the close of the case for the prosecution may address the jury in his behalf. And here I must impress upon you the difference of the proof required between the parties in a civil and in a criminal case. In the former the dispute is between subject and subject, and the object is to obtain all the facts in the readiest manner. Both sides must give evidence, or it will be presumed that what one deposes to must be true because it is not refuted by the other. In a criminal case it is vastly different. All the power of the State is employed against the accused; the Crown is prosecutor, and has unlimited sums of money and resources at its command, to collect evidence, secure the attendance of witnesses, and to obtain men of the highest rank at the bar to conduct the case. Therefore, as the first object of the law is to protect the weak against the strong, it throws every possible shield around the accused against the abuse of power. He is not bound to criminate himself; it is for the prosecution to prove his guilt, not for him to prove his innocence. He may not be heard upon oath to contradict, or explain, what has been deposed to by his prosecutors; therefore the case against him must be made out beyond any doubt such as would occur to the mind of a reasonable man, or he is entitled to his acquittal.

The direct contrary of these wholesome provisions appears to prevail in many continental States. There, the prosecution starts with the assumption that the prisoner is guilty, and calls upon him to prove his innocence. He is cross-examined by his judges with the view of getting him to make admissions from which his guilt may be inferred. Poor and ignorant as the great majority of those accused of crime in all countries are, it is an easy task for a practised mind to wring from the most guiltless person, by this process of mental torture, some contradiction or equivocation that may condemn him. Every act of his life is raked up against him, and it is sought to prove that he committed the offence for which he is being tried, by showing that at some other time he was found guilty of something that has nothing whatever to do with it! Worst of all, he may be tried and convicted in his absence upon a charge of which he may be utterly ignorant. The cruelty and bad policy of a system which shuts out reformation to the convicted, is apparent. Our law is more just and logical. It does not seek to find a man guilty of murder because, when a boy, he stole apples; but our neighbours across the Channel would gravely state that fact in the indictment. They prove previous convictions against a prisoner at the *outset* of his trial. We allow them to be mentioned only after it is concluded. With us a jury are sworn to give a true verdict *according to the evidence*, and none is admitted that does not directly bear upon the issue to be tried. I have no doubt but that you have heard it complained of that some crafty fellow has escaped punishment by a mere *quibble of law*, but you never hear how that same "quibble" may have protected innocent persons from untrue and malicious charges. Better, say I, that a hundred criminals should escape—they are sure to get their due some day—than that one honest man should suffer.

It is not necessary that a prisoner should be *seen* to commit a crime before he can be convicted of it. There are presumptions of fact, upon which jurors are justified in deciding; for example, if a man be found near the place where a murder has been committed, with his hands stained with blood, having in his possession a weapon such as might have been used to do the deed, a jury would no doubt find him guilty, unless he could explain away these circumstances. Or, if a person be discovered in possession of stolen goods immediately after they have been stolen, and fails to give a reasonable account of how he came by them, the natural conclusion must be that he is the thief.

I will now return to the proceedings at a criminal trial. The case for the Crown having been closed, the presiding judge asks the counsel for the defence (supposing there be one) whether he intends to call witnesses on behalf of the prisoner. If he reply in the negative, the counsel for the prosecution sums up his evidence; and the prisoner's counsel then addresses the jury. If, on the contrary, witnesses are called for the defence, the counsel for the prosecution does not sum up his evidence, but has a general reply at the close of the case; the prisoner's counsel having the right previously to sum up the evidence he has adduced. When the Attorney-General appears in a criminal case, he has a right to reply, whether evidence be given for the prisoner or not. No Queen's counsel may accept a brief to defend a prisoner without a licence from the Crown, to obtain which a fee must be paid, of course by the person requiring his assistance. The reason for this rule is, that Queen's counsel must all hold themselves in readiness to act for the Crown, and may be called upon at any time to conduct the prosecutions taken in her Majesty's name.

When both sides have been heard, the presiding judge sums up the evidence to the jury, who return a verdict of "guilty" or "not guilty," according to the evidence. If the former, the prisoner is sentenced according to law; if the latter, he is discharged. The same rule which governs civil proceedings prevails; the judge lays down the law, and the jury decide upon the facts. If a legal question of sufficient difficulty arise, the judge "reserves the point" for the consideration of the Court of Criminal Appeal, which is composed of all the superior judges; and, pending their decision, according to circumstances, the prisoner is remanded or admitted to bail.

The result of the trial is entered on the indictment which forms the "record" of the case. If a substantial defect appear in this, what is called a "writ of error" may be obtained, with the consent of the Attorney-General, which is granted as a matter of course. The prisoner then appears in person in the Court of Queen's Bench and "assigns error"—that is, states formally in writing the mistakes upon which he relies, and demands to be acquitted. The Attorney-General makes "joinder in error," denying that the record and proceedings are faulty; the question comes on for argument, and the judgment is either affirmed or reversed, according to law.

No new trial can be obtained upon a mistake in *fact*, even if it be clearly ascertained after the trial that the witnesses on either side have been guilty of perjury, or have been mistaken, or that others can be brought to prove or disprove any doubtful particular. If it appear that the prisoner has been wrongly convicted, the royal prerogative of pardon is exercised, and he is released. If, on the other hand, he be wrongfully acquitted, there is no resource, for, as I have told you, no person can be tried a second time for the same offence. You will easily perceive that this is a great defect in our law; it is but a poor consolation to a person who has been proclaimed a felon in open court to receive in secret, through the post, a pardon for a crime he has never committed. The pardon should, at any rate, be granted as publicly as the sentence was pronounced.

LETTER XVIII.

THE LAW OF EVIDENCE.

Conditions of Evidence — Parol — Verbal — Direct — Circumstantial — Primary and Secondary Evidence.

You now know how civil and criminal trials are conducted; but there is a very important subject respecting which I must give you some information before I conclude—that is, the law of evidence, which regulates what sort of testimony may or may not be received.

Evidence is so called because it makes *evident* the point in issue. It is of two kinds, *parol*, or verbal, and *written*. These, again, are divided into *primary* and *secondary* evidence.

Parol evidence is that which is given by word of mouth by witnesses. It is usually given upon oath; and formerly Quakers, Moravians, and others who are forbidden by their religion to take one, although they might give evidence upon affirmation in a civil action, were incompetent to give testimony in a Criminal Court. By a recent Act of

Parliament this distinction is abolished, and persons who have conscientious objections to being sworn may make an affirmation that what they are about to say is the truth; after which, their evidence is admitted. It is a general rule that persons must be sworn in the manner most binding upon their conscience. Thus, the Christian is sworn upon the New Testament with his head uncovered; the Jew upon the five books of Moses, with his hat on; the Mahometan upon the Koran; the Hindoo by the river Ganges; the Chinese by breaking a saucer, and praying that he may be similarly destroyed if he be guilty of a falsehood. Idiots, lunatics, and children who do not understand the nature of an oath, cannot be admitted to give evidence.

Husband and wife may not be witnesses for or against each other in criminal cases, except when a charge of bigamy is to be proved, and in some cases where the wife accuses her husband of having injured her or deprived her of her liberty.

Prisoners upon their trial may not be examined upon oath upon their own behalf, but if several persons be jointly indicted, any one of them may be called as a witness either for or against his co-defendants, excepting only in those few cases where the indictment is so framed as to give him a direct interest in obtaining their discharge.

Evidence may be given by persons who have been previously convicted of crimes, but such testimony is always received with suspicion. Witnesses may only state what they know of their own knowledge; what they have heard from others is not evidence, because its accuracy depends upon the truth of the speaker, and he is not upon his oath. But if the person to whom the words related was within hearing, and had an opportunity of contradicting them and did not do so, then the person who heard what was said may give it in evidence, for the silence of him to whom it related is considered as an admission that it was true. The *best* or *primary* evidence must always be given. Thus, the contents of a written document may not be heard upon *parol*, or a copy of it admitted, because the document itself provides the best evidence of what is stated in it. But if it be a writing such as from its position cannot be brought into court—an inscription upon a wall for example—a verbal account of its contents or a drawing of it may be admitted. In *pedigree* cases, and some other, in which *reputation* is the only proof that can be given, *hearsay* or *secondary* evidence may be given. Thus, entries in old Bibles, recitals in deeds, dates and particulars on ancient coffin-plates, &c. &c., are received as evidence

Written evidence is proof by the production of written records or documents.

An examined copy of, or extract from, many papers of a public character may be admitted to prove a fact; and if such as are of a private nature happen to be in the custody, or under the control, of the adverse party, upon giving him *notice to produce it*, and his neglecting or refusing to do so, a copy or counterpart may be used as secondary evidence, or part testimony may be given of its contents.

Evidence thus composed is either *direct* or *circumstantial*. Direct evidence is such as plainly proves that a person did or said something. Circumstantial evidence is a combination of circumstances from which it may be inferred that he did so. I have already given you some instances of this latter kind of proof in my letter upon the criminal procedure. The former requires no description. The admissibility or non-admissibility of evidence is a question for the judge. Its value in determining the issue, remains for the jury to consider.

I have given you but an imperfect outline of this important subject in the space which is left me. Half the discussions in our courts turn upon the law of evidence, and its study is one of the principal labours of those who follow the legal profession. But I trust, however, I have said enough to make you understand what is meant, when you hear some statement which to the uninitiated may appear to be conclusive proof, objected to in a court of justice as *not being evidence.*

LETTER XIX.

CONCLUSION.

I MUST now draw our correspondence to an end, not because I have exhausted the subject upon which I have touched, but because I have gone as far as is for the present desirable. It has been a labour of love to me, and to you, I hope, it will be a source not only of amusement, but instruction. I trust that the little information which I have imparted will only make you thirst to acquire more knowledge respecting the progress of our glorious constitution, and the theory and practice of a law which, taking it all in all, is the soundest in principle, and in practice the purest of any code, ancient or modern. In the politics of parties and the fate of cabinets you cannot, at your ages, be expected to feel much interest; but every girl and boy in England ought to know the great value of the rights which they inherit; and what can be a more fascinating study than to trace through the pages of Blackstone, Hallam, or Macaulay, or De Lolme, the struggles, sacrifices, and triumphs of the brave and good men who won and protected these rights for us?

It is the fashion, nevertheless, with a certain class of our public writers and speakers to cry down the institutions of their country and to applaud to the echo those of foreign States. They may be perfectly conscientious in what they advance; but they are evidently too ready to expose the faults of our system, and not so willing to acknowledge the benefits which ought, in common fairness, to be set off against them. Such reasoners are too prone to fall into raptures at what they have seen, or heard of, abroad, after a very superficial examination. Strike a fair balance, and what country under the sun is so free, so happy, so secure as our own? We have a Queen upon the throne who, as a monarch, is an example to every crowned head, and as a Christian gentlewoman, a pattern to every fireside. We have an aristocracy that has learned to carry its pride without offence, and is ever active in its endeavours to do something for the people in return for the privileges which it enjoys. We have a middle class that is raising imperishable monuments to its own industry and enterprise in every quarter of the globe. We have strong, honest workmen, without whose skill and strength those monuments would never rise. We have Poor honourably and bravely toiling, Poor ignorant and starving, Poor vicious and degraded, but I think that there are few amongst the community at large that are not adding their mite to the great work of encouraging, educating, providing for, and reforming them.

Can we look abroad to find that a better government than our own exists? No; with all its faults and short-comings—and they are many—the British Constitution stands pre-eminent amidst the ruling systems of the world. That this may long continue to be the case must be the fervent prayer of every loyal and patriotic Englishman, as it is of

Your affectionate father,
A. B.

INDEX.

ACCESSARIES—See *Principals*
Actions, forms of, 152; costs of, 161; proceedings in, 154; pleadings in, 154; parties in, 152
Address to the Crown, 50
Admirals, gradations of, 132
Admiralty, Board of, 128; First Lord of, 128; powers of, 128
Adjutant-General, duties of, 100
Aldermen, 79
Ancient Warfare, 97
Appropriation Bill, 58
Appeal, court of Criminal, 198; Supreme court of, 30; from Superior courts, 159; in Bankruptcy, 163; in Equity, 160
Archdeacons, 89
Army, the British—composition of, 101; designation of regiments in, 112; expense of, 115; quarters and encampments of, 105; recruited, how, 109; strength of, 115; standing, origin of, 97
Articles of War, 99
Arson, crime of, 169
Artillery, introduction of, 97; importance of, 113; Foot, strength of, 113; Horse, strength of, 113
Assaults, 170
Assisting a prisoner to escape, offence of, 170
Attorney, what, 153; how admitted to practice, 152
Attorney-General, the, 47
Autrefois acquit, plea of, 175
Autrefois convict, plea of, 175
BALANCE OF TRADE, 68
Ballot, the, 40
Bankruptcy, appeals in, 163; courts of, 162; judges in ditto, 163; practice of ditto, 163
Baron, rank of, 5—8, 29
Barristers, how called to the Bar, 152
Bath, Order of the, 117
Bigamy, crime of, 169
Bill in Parliament, 56; opposing a, 56; passing a, 53—55; public, 52; private, 52—57
Bill of Rights, the, 12

INDEX. 209

Bishop, derivation of title of, 87 ; how chosen, 87 ; right to sit in Parliament, 28 ; trials of, 176
Board of Trade, President of, 46
Board of Admiralty, duties of, 128
Boards of Health, 79
Boroughs, one of the divisions of the country into, 71
Borough-mongers, what, 33
Budget, the, 57
Burgesses, 9
Burglary, crime of, 168
CABINET COUNCIL, 44
Candidates for election in Parliament, disqualifications of, 37
Canterbury, province of, 86 ; suffragan bishops in, 87
Challenges to jurors, 192
Chancellor of the Exchequer, 46 ; the Lord High Chancellor, 45, 161
Cheating, offence of, 170
Chiltern Hundreds, the, 42
Church accommodation, 92
Church of England, history of, 80
Churchwardens, origin and duties of, 73, 75
Circuits of the Judges, 150
Circumstantial evidence, 203
Civil Law, the, 142, 143
Civil List, the, 21
Coast-Guard, the, 140
Coast Volunteers, the, 141
Coining, offence of, 169
Commissary-General, 101
Committee of House of Commons, 54 ; Select, 57 ; of Supply, 58 ; of Ways and Means, 58
Common Council-men, 79
Common law, the, 142
Common Pleas, Court of, 148
Commons, House of, 31 ; composition of, 35 ; rights of, 42 ; voting in, 56 ; Speaker of, 49 ; proceedings in, 50
Commune Concilium Regni, the, 4
Consolidated Fund, the, 20
Conspiracy, offence of, 171
Constitution, definition and origin of British, 3
Constable, duties of, 71*
Convocation, what, 91
Coroner, office and duties of, 178
Corporations, Municipal, 78
Costs, in actions and suits, 161 ; in criminal cases, 173
Country, divisions of the, 71
County Courts, the, 161
Courts of Law, definition of, 148 ; of Bankruptcy, 162 ; Central

Criminal, the, 180 ; of Common Pleas, 148 ; of Criminal Appeal, 198 ; District Courts of Record, 151 ; of Equity, 162 ; of Exchequer, 148 ; of the Lord High Steward, 177 ; Martial, 116, 139 ; of Oyer and Terminer and gaol delivery, 179 ; of Parliament, 176 ; of Police, 182 ; of Queen's Bench, 148, 177 ; of Quarter Sessions, 181
Crimes and offences, classification of, 165
Criminal law and practice, 183 ; Foreign, how conducted, 195
Curates, 89
DAMAGES, 158—160
Deacons, ordination of, and title to orders of, 91
Dean and Chapter, 88
Depositions, what, 185
Duke, definition of title of, 28
EARL, derivation of title of, 29
Election of Members of Parliament, before the Reform Act, 32 ; after, 39 ; expenses of, 40 ; proceedings at, 39
Electors, qualification of, 36
Embezzlement, crime of, 170
Engineers, the Royal, 114
Equity, what, 143 ; conflicts of, with law, 144 ; courts of, 160 ; judges in, 160 ; old procedure in, 145 ; new, 145
Escaping from prison, offence of, 170
Evidence, circumstantial, 203 ; law of, 200 ; hearsay, 202 ; parol, 200 ; written, 203
Exchequer, Court of, 148
Exports, British, amount of, 68
FALSE Weights and Scales, offence of using, 171
Felony, what now is, 165, 168 ; costs of prosecuting, 173 ; when committed by drunkards, idiots, married women, and infants, 174
Feudal system, the, 5, 95
Feuds, division of the kingdom into, 5
Fines on land, &c., under feudal system, 6
First Lord of the Admiralty, 46, 128
First Lord of the Treasury, 45
Flags in the Army, 113
Foreign prosecutions contrasted with English, 195
Foreigners, trials of, 187
Forgery, crime of, 169
Freeholders, origin of term of, 7
Funds, 61
GAMBLING, offence of, 171
Government bills, 52—57
Government of England defined, 16
Grand Jury, functions of, 187
Greenwich Hospital, 138
Guards, the, 101 ; brevet rank in, 109

HEALTH, Boards of, 79
Hearsay evidence, 202
High treason, 166; punishment for, 166
Highways, surveyors of, 73
Housebreaking, crime of, 169
Houses of Parliament—See *Commons and Peers.*
Household troops, 101, 102
Hundreds, divisions of the country into, 71
Hustings at elections, where erected, 39

IMPORTS, British, amount of, 68
Improvement Commissioners, 79
Incumbent clergy, 89
Indictments, 186, 190
Informations, 191
Inns of Court, the, 152
Inquisition and inquest—See *Coroner.*
Irish peers, and members of Parliament, 26, 35

JEWS, former disabilities of, 85
Judges—See *Courts of Law,* &c.
Judicial Committee of Privy Council, 44
Jurors, challenges to, 192
Jury, grand, the, 187; common or petty, the 155; mixed, for the trial of foreigners, 185; qualifications for serving on, 155; special, 156
Justices of the Peace, 71*, 179, 181

KNIGHTS of the shire, 9

LARCENY, 170
Law, the, administration of, 145—148; common, the, 142; civil, the, 143; criminal, the, 143, 183; execution of, 146; interpretation of, 145; statute, the, 142; superior courts of, 148
Libels, 171
Local government, 70
Lords, House of—See *Peers.*
Lord Lieutenant, 71
Lord Privy Seal, the, 46

Magnum Concilium Regis, the, 4
Maintenance of the poor, 74
Manslaughter, crime of, 167
Marines, the Royal, 141
Marquess, derivation of title of, 28
Marriage Act, the Royal, 24
Married women, felony by, 174
Medals for victories, 118
Members of Parliament, how elected, 38; unseating, and expulsion of, 41; numbers of, 35; qualifications of, 37; ministerial, 47; opposition, 48
Mercenary soldiers, 96

Michel Gemote, the, 4
Michel Synod, the, 4
Militia, the 119, 120
Ministry, the, how composed, 45—48
Misdemeanours, 170, 174
Money, price of, 63
Municipal Corporations, 78
Mutiny Act, 58
Murder, crime of, 167; attempting to commit, 168
NATIONAL Debt, the, 59—67
Navy—See *Royal Navy*
Naval Reserve, Royal, 141
Nobility—See *Peers*
Norman Conquest, consequences of, 5
Nuisances, 174
OATH, mode of taking an, 200
Officers—See *Army, Navy, Marines*, and *Militia*
Opposition, the Parliamentary, 47
Order of the Bath, 117
Order of St. Michael and St. George, 118
PARDONS to convicted persons, 199
Parishes, division of the country into, 71
Parliament (see also *Commons* and *Peers*), assembly of, 38; duration of, 38; opening of, by the Queen, 50; by Commission, 51; passing a Bill in, 53; proceedings in, 51, 53; official printing Reports of, 52; admission of strangers in, 51
Parol evidence, 200
Paymaster-General of the Army, 101
Peers, House of, 8; creation of, 29; privileges of, 30; protest by dissentient, 30; proxies of, 30; trials of, 177
Pensioners in the army, 118; in the navy, 138
Penance, old punishment of, *peine forte et dure*, 188
Perjury, crime of, 170
Piracy, crime of, 169
Pleading, in criminal cases, 188; in civil actions, 153
Poaching, offence of, 171
Police Courts, 185
Poll at elections, 40
Poor, maintenance of, 74
Poor Law, origin of, 74; old and present laws, 76, 77.
Pope of Rome, authority of, in this country, 81
Postmaster-General, 46
Practice of criminal law, 183; of civil law, 148
Prerogative of the Crown, 18
President of the Board of Trade, 46
Presumptions of criminality, 197
Priests, ordination of, 91
Primary evidence, 202

INDEX.   213

Prince of Wales, the, 23
Princess Royal, the, 23
Principals and accessaries, 173
Privy Council, the, 43 ; Cabinet Council of, 44 ; Judicial Committee of, 44
Privy Councillor, oath of, 43 ; power of, 44 ; title of, 45
Privy Seal, the Lord, 46
Proceedings at criminal trials, 186 ; in civil actions, 154—164
Proroguing of Parliament, 58
Public prosecutor, supposed necessity for, 183
Purchase system in the army, 105
Puritans, former disabilities of, 83
QUEEN CONSORT, the, 23
Queen Dowager, the, 23
Queen's Counsel require licence to defend prisoners, 197
Queen's Advocate, 47
Queen's Bench, Court of, 148, 177
Quartermaster-General, 101
RATES, of what kind, and how levied, 71*
Rating of ships in the navy, 129
Receiving stolen goods, crime of, 170
Record in criminal cases, what, 198 ; in civil cases, 155
Recruit, how enlisted, and bounty to, 109, 110
Rector, what kind of living held by, 89
Reformers, political, 33
Religious disabilities of Roman Catholics, Puritans, Dissenters, and Jews, 83—85
Revenue, amount of, at various times, 67
Rights of Englishmen, 12
Rioting, offence of, 170
Robbery, crime of, 168
Roman Catholics, former disabilities of, 84 ; since repealed, 85
Rotten boroughs, 33
Royal assent to Bills in Parliament, 55
Royal Consort, the, 22
Royal Family, the, 22
Royal Navy, the history of, 122 ; officers of, their pay, 133 ; their commissions, 137 ; their number (1865), 137 ; their relative rank, 136 ; warrant officers, their pay, 138 ; cadets in, 141 ; pensioners in, 139 ; discipline of the navy, 140 ; how manned, 137 ; iron ships and batteries, 131 ; direction of affairs of, 127 ; triumphs of, 126
Rural deans, 89
SCOTCH PEERS, and Members of Parliament, 26, 35
Secondary evidence, 202
Secretary of State for War, 46, 100 ; for the Colonies, 46 ; for Home Department, 46 ; for India, 46 ; for Foreign Affairs, 46
Select Committees of Houses of Parliament, 57

Serjeants-at-Law, 152
Sheriff, High, 71, 146; under, or deputy, 147
Shires, divisions of the country into, 71
Show of hands at elections, 39
Sinking Fund, 64
Smuggling, 171
Soldiers; how the common soldier is enlisted, 109; pay of, 110; prospects of, and promotion of, 110
Solicitor-General, 47
Speaker of House of Commons, 41; election of, 49; salary of, 50
Speaker of House of Lords, 29
Special jury, 156
Special case, what, 160
Stabbing, crime of, 168
Statute Law, the 142
Statutes, construction of, 198
St. Michael and St. George, Order of, 118
Succession to the throne of Great Britain, the, 17
Surveyors of highways, 73
Tenant in capite, what, 6
Threatening letters, offence of sending, 171
Tithes, 90
Tithings, division of the country into, 71
Towns, formation of, 9
Trade, balance of, 68
Transportation, returning from, 170; offence of, 172; punishment of, now abolished, 172
Trial, civil cases, 156; criminal ditto, 193
UTTERING forged documents, 169; base coin, 171
VASSAL, what, 5
Verdict of the Jury, 158, 198
Vestry, 73
Vicar, in the Church of England, 89
Victoria Cross, Order of Valour, 118
Viscount, derivation of title of, 29
Volunteers, 121
WITTENA GEMOTE, the, 4
Witness, who may be a, 200
Writ of error, 198
Written evidence, 203.
YEOMANRY, the, 121
York, province of, 86; suffragan bishops of, 87

THE END.

www.ingramcontent.com/pod-product-compliance
Lightning Source LLC
Chambersburg PA
CBHW031813230426
43669CB00009B/1129